D0828347

DISCARD

MAR 2016

Westminster Public Library
3705 W. 112th Ave.
Westminster, CO 80031
www.westminsterlibrary.org

MARTHA WASHINGTON

Legendary First Lady of the United States

Stephanie Sammartino McPherson

Enslow Publishers, Inc.
40 Industrial Road
Box 398
Berkeley Heights, NJ 07922
USA
http://www.enslow.com

Dedication

For Jennie Zanghi and Marie McPherson, who shared
Martha Washington's courage and commitment to family

Copyright © 2015 by Stephanie Sammartino McPherson

All rights reserved.

Originally published as *Martha Washington: First Lady* in 1998.

No part of this book may be reproduced by any means without the written permission of the publisher.

Library of Congress Cataloging-in-Publication Data
McPherson, Stephanie Sammartino.
  Martha Washington : legendary First Lady of the United States / Stephanie Sammartino McPherson.
    pages cm. — (Legendary American biographies)
  "Originally published as Martha Washington: First Lady in 1998."
  Includes bibliographical references and index.
  ISBN ISBN 978-0-7660-6475-1 (library bound) — ISBN 978-0-7660-6476-8 (pbk.)—ISBN 978-0-7660-6477-5 (epub.) 1. Washington, Martha, 1731–1802—juvenile literature. 2. Presidents' spouses—United States—Biography—Juvenile literature. 3. United States—Politics and governmen—1789–1797—Juvenile literature. 4. Washington, George, 1732–1799—Juvenile literature. I. Title.
  E312.19.M37 2015
  973.4'1092—dc23
  [B]
                                    2014029272
Future editions:
Paperback ISBN: 978-0-7660-6476-8   Single-User PDF ISBN: 978-0-7660-6478-2
EPUB ISBN: 978-0-7660-6477-5   Multi-User PDF ISBN: 978-0-7660-6479-9

Printed in the United States of America
102014 Bang Printing, Brainerd, Minn.
10 9 8 7 6 5 4 3 2 1

To Our Readers: We have done our best to make sure all Internet addresses in this book were active and appropriate when we went to press. However, the author and the publisher have no control over and assume no liability for the material available on those Internet sites or on other Web sites they may link to. Send comments by e-mail to comments@enslow.com or to the address on the back cover.

✪ Enslow Publishers, Inc., is committed to printing our books on recycled paper. The paper in every book contains 10% to 30% post-consumer waste (PCW). The cover board on the outside of each book contains 100% PCW. Our goal is to do our part to help young people and the environment too!

Illustration Credits: ©Clipart.com, p. 6; Shutterstock.com: ©A-R-T (scrolls)

Cover Illustration Credit: Library of Congress

CONTENTS

ACKNOWLEDGMENTS

I would especially like to thank Angelo Sammartino for profound help in sorting through historical details and for being the first to review the manuscript; Frank Grizzard, assistant editor of The Papers of George Washington Project at the University of Virginia, for the penetrating assessment of historical accuracy and sources; and Richard McPherson for his untiring support and encouragement.

Special thanks go to Robert Durden, Jennifer McPherson, Marianne McPherson, Edith Fine, Judith Josephson, Karen Coombs, Suzan Wilson, Barbara McMillan of the Mount Vernon Ladies' Association, and the library staff of the Virginia Historical Society. I would also like to thank Susan Berquist, for sharing her historical interpretation of Martha Washington, and Mary Wiseman of the Colonial Williamsburg Foundation.

I am indebted to the following for help with photo research: Lee Vivarette and Audrey Johnson of the Library of Virginia, Julie Cline of Washington and Lee University, Doris Delk and Ann Marie Price of the Virginia Historical Society, Joni Rowe and Theresa Vazquez of the National Park Service, Karen Tates-Denton of the Brooklyn Museum, and Karen Van Epps Peters of the Mount Vernon Ladies' Association.

Author's Note

When Martha Washington burned her papers before her death, she created a host of problems for biographers. Before her marriage to George Washington, there is little record of the events in her life. Traditions that have been handed down cannot always be verified, and sometimes historians dispute them. Weighing the evidence, I have chosen what seemed in each case to be the most likely scenario.

Although the details of her life are somewhat obscured, there can be no doubt about Martha Washington's character. Whether interacting with slaves or foreign statesmen, family friends or her grandchildren, she had a directness and warmth that drew people to her. It requires just a little imagination to determine how a committed and courageous individual would react to the situations that faced Martha Washington.

George Washington dominates the national consciousness so much that it becomes almost impossible to refer to his wife by her surname alone even in her own biography. The name Washington instantly summons up pictures of the general on horseback or the president in all his dignity. Since first-name usage seems to diminish Martha Washington's place in American history, both her first and her surname are used throughout this book.

This portrait was done of Martha Dandridge Custis, shortly after her marriage to Daniel Parke Custis in 1750.

Chapter 1

PATTERN OF INDUSTRY

Guns exploded as the stout, middle-aged woman reached the front door. Entering the house, she spied a frantic girl racing down the stairs. "The British are coming!" cried the young woman.[1]

Calmly, the visitor gathered Susan Boudinot in her arms. The British were not coming, the older woman explained. The shots they heard were just American soldiers practicing for battle.

The tension in the room evaporated instantly. A familiar and cherished guest in the Boudinot household, Martha Washington had never been more welcome.

A Dangerously Small Army

Everywhere she went, people welcomed Martha Washington that spring of 1777. She had arrived in March at Morristown, New Jersey, where General George Washington and his troops were camped for the winter. During the cold weather most fighting ceased, and wives could join their husbands until hostilities began again in the spring. This was the second time Martha Washington had joined her husband during the Revolutionary War, and it was far different from her previous experience in Cambridge, Massachusetts. There, she had been relatively safe and comfortable. Here, she felt much closer to the war and the suffering soldiers.

Despite the seasonal lull, some fighting continued as small bands of American soldiers challenged British scouting parties. The Americans did well in these skirmishes, but Martha Washington knew the general did not want to provoke a full-scale attack. The American Army was simply too small to stand up to the entire British Army.

Brave Deeds

With so much uncertainty and danger, General Washington had delayed sending for his wife this year. He did not want to expose her to such risks. However, Martha Washington was more concerned for her husband's well-being than her own. While she had endured a lonely holiday at Mount Vernon in Virginia, the general and his men had spent Christmas night marching through a blizzard to a ferry landing on the Delaware River. Huddled on swirling barges and navigating between chunks of ice, the army crossed to the opposite shore in New Jersey. By the first week of January 1777, the Americans had won two battles and had driven the British from Trenton and Princeton. Relieved at the news, Martha Washington wondered if her husband would now ask for her company at winter headquarters.

At last, the summons arrived, and Martha Washington headed north. When she arrived in Philadelphia, the military escort that met her gave her distressing news.[2] George Washington had become seriously ill with a fever and sore throat. Before modern medicines, such an ailment could prove deadly. Anxiously, Martha Washington pressed forward on her journey.

Joyful Meeting

Several miles from the camp, her carriage stopped at a home. The general himself hurried out to greet her. Five-foot Martha Washington looked up in relief and joy at her six-foot-two-inch husband. Perhaps she even grabbed him by his lapels and pulled him closer to her level as she sometimes did when she had something urgent to say.[3] George Washington looked weary, even haggard, but the worst was over, and he was starting to regain his strength. For the moment, that was all that mattered to his wife.

As soon as she reached the tavern that served as headquarters, Martha Washington set to work to make the general more comfortable. Her strength of character and bustling cheerfulness were a source of comfort and stability to the worried general. "[General Washington's] worthy lady seems in perfect felicity by the side of her 'Old Man,' as she calls him," one observer

Arnold's Tavern

It is believed that Arnold's Tavern served as George Washington's first Morristown headquarters. The public dance hall could hold large staff meetings, and the second floor had a front room for official business and a back room for the general's private quarters.[4]

noted.[5] As George Washington's health improved, he and his wife rode together on horseback, often with some of his military aides. Privately, Martha Washington shared all the news from home and listened to her husband speak about his frustration at the dwindling size of his army and his worries about the troops' health.

Smallpox ravaged the camp. A church had to be turned into a hospital to house the sick and to inoculate the well against the often deadly disease. Inoculation was a risky procedure in the eighteenth century. At best, those inoculated would suffer a mild form of the illness; at worst, they would die. By mid-March, one third of the troops at Morristown were sick from the inoculation.[6] The remaining soldiers suffered, too, as they trudged through the snow in thin, tattered clothing and worn-out shoes. They were lonely and discouraged.

Inspiration to Others

Martha Washington felt deeply for the ragged young men, some the same age as her own son. Whenever possible, she brought them soup, medicine, and shirts or stockings. The soldiers responded to her kindness and gentle ways. The fact that the wife of their commander in chief, a fine lady used to a grand plantation, would choose to spend her winter at camp meant a great deal. Spirits rose whenever Mrs. Washington came to call.[7]

Martha Washington's presence also excited much interest among the local families and the wives of other military officers. But when several Morristown ladies decided to visit her, they learned she was quite different from what they expected. One woman recalled the incident with embarrassment: "As she was said to be so grand a lady, we thought we must put on our best bibs and bands. So we dressed ourselves in our most elegant ruffles and silks."[8] To their surprise and chagrin, the ladies found

Martha Washington in a simple brown dress and a checked apron. She greeted her guests cheerfully, then picked up her knitting needles to work on a pair of stockings.

Matter-of-factly, Martha Washington explained that American women now had to produce items that were previously imported from England. She declared, "We must become independent by our determination to do without what we cannot make ourselves. Whilst our husbands and brothers are examples of patriotism, we must be patterns of industry!"[9]

Martha Washington had made Mount Vernon as independent as possible. By her own account "sixteen spinning-wheels were kept in constant operation."[10] Her homemade dresses were plain, but she was proud of them. Once, at Mount Vernon, she showed off two dresses made of cotton and silk. Refusing to import new English silk, Martha Washington had obtained her fabric from "the ravellings of brown silk stockings and old crimson damask chaircovers."[11]

The women of Morristown responded to Martha Washington's intense patriotism and genuine warmth. "She seems very wise in experience, kind-hearted and winning in all her ways," one visitor wrote. "She talked much of the poor soldiers, especially the sick ones. Her heart seems to be full of compassion for them."[12]

Martha Washington stayed at Morristown as long as the general would permit. In late May, however, rumors reached camp that the British might be planning to march on Philadelphia. George Washington thought it best for her to leave before any fighting occurred.

Leaving her husband to return home was difficult for Martha Washington. She did not complain, but she must have dreaded the uncertainty that came with the separation. She had spent less than three months with her husband and did not know when—or even if—she would see him again. The general might be captured by the British and hanged as a traitor. He might be killed on the battlefield. Martha Washington knew that the American cause meant more to her husband than personal safety. Determined to be an example to his men, General Washington rode boldly into battle, an easy target for enemy fire.

It took a different kind of bravery for Martha Washington to bid a calm good-bye to her husband that spring. Resolutely, she stepped into the carriage with her son, to begin her journey home.

Chapter 2

MARTHA
DANDRIDGE CUSTIS

L ong before she had ever heard of Mount Vernon, home for Martha Dandridge was a comfortable plantation house on the shore of the Pamunkey River near Williamsburg, then the capital of Virginia. Chestnut Grove was not a grand house, but it had large fireplaces, a convenient kitchen in the basement, and good-sized rooms on the first and second floors. Martha was born there on June 2, 1731, the first of nine children born to John and Frances Orlando Jones Dandridge. Martha's father, a gentleman farmer and clerk of New Kent County, had come to the American colonies from England seventeen years earlier. Her mother, the granddaughter of a minister, grew up in Williamsburg.

Although little is known about Martha's girlhood, the life of a plantation child was a privileged and usually happy one. Nicknamed Patcy, Martha grew up surrounded by green fields, loving parents, and friendly neighbors. When she was very young, she played with her dolls, learned her alphabet, and watched the tobacco ripen through the seasons. Almost certainly she went with her father and mother to visit Williamsburg. A twenty-five-mile trip was an adventure in the 1730s, but her parents had business associates and relatives in the city, which made the long trip worth it. The Dandridges probably traveled by boat, following the turns of the Pamunkey River to the York and landing in Queen's Creek, just one mile from Williamsburg.[1]

There the fun began. Peering into shops on fashionable Duke of Gloucester Street, Martha noted such fascinating items as snuffboxes, fancy buttons, dolls, pinwheels, quill pens, and powder for mixing ink. In the mantua (dressmaker) shop, she could see the latest "fashion babies," tiny mannequins dressed in elegant doll-sized gowns. Every shop created its own charmed world, from the silversmith to the wigmaker to the apothecary who sold potions and powders for a variety of ills. In Publick Times, the period when elected officials met, Martha might see grand carriages and men in powdered wigs bustling in and out of the Capitol.

Chestnut Grove may have seemed tame compared with the excitement of Williamsburg, but it was home. Martha, surrounded by brothers and sisters, had little time to be lonely. She welcomed neighbors, visited nearby plantations, and probably enjoyed the barbecues and fish feasts so popular in colonial Virginia.

Education

Preparation for festive occasions took time and effort. Martha's daily routine was full as she learned to manage household affairs and to entertain graciously. Unlike her brothers, who were preparing to deal with business and civic affairs, Martha was learning to take her place in polite society. Although she studied with her brothers' tutor, Martha got little from her sessions beyond the basics of reading, writing, and arithmetic. She never

Building a Capital

In 1698, the Virginia statehouse at Jamestown burned down. This was the fourth fire in the legislative building, and it gave Virginians the excuse they needed to finally move their state capital away from swampy Jamestown. Legislators chose a settlement on high ground between two rivers as their new capital. The existing town was very small, giving planners free rein to create the new capital from scratch. In honor of King William III of England, the name of the village was changed from Middle Plantation to Williamsburg.

completely mastered spelling or the finer points of grammar, a deficiency that would embarrass her later in life. But girls were not expected to equal their brothers' classroom performance. Martha's most important teacher was her mother, who taught her how to cook, sew, and do fancy embroidery. By all accounts, Martha was talented with a needle. She also tended the kitchen garden, learning what spices to use in recipes and what herbs to use as medicines.[2]

As she went about her daily tasks, Martha saw her father's slaves harvest tobacco in the fields, clean the house, and care for horses in the stables. Their work seemed endless, but few people in eighteenth-century America questioned the justice of the slavery system. Martha, though kind to the domestics and field-workers, grew up taking slavery for granted.

Although she generally did what was expected of her, Martha did have spirited moments. According to one legend, she rode her horse Fatima up the stairway to the veranda of her uncle's house. This was certainly not proper behavior for the future mistress of a plantation, and her mother and aunt began to reprimand her. But Martha's father, impressed by the feat, would not hear a word against Martha. "Let Patcy alone!" he exclaimed. "She's not harmed William's staircase. And, by heavens, how she can ride!"[3]

Whatever the factual basis for this tale, Mrs. Dandridge was more concerned with ladylike behavior than with riding. Martha took dancing lessons from traveling masters who taught her the latest steps. The dancing teacher's arrival meant a holiday from the schoolroom but not from hard work and concentration. As one historian has noted, "The children had to go through their paces with precision and grace, for the dancing master demanded as strict a discipline on the dance floor as the tutor did in the schoolroom."[4] The same diligence probably kept Martha at the piano for long hours, learning another prized social skill.

Conversation was also considered an art.[5] Although sometimes shy, Martha took to this art naturally. She cared about people in a way that made it almost impossible not to like her. By age fifteen, she was ready (and probably quite eager) to make her entrance into Virginia society.

Courtship

The governor's ball in Williamsburg was the highlight of the Virginia social season. Martha mingled with the most fashionable ladies and gentlemen in the colony. Perhaps this is where she first came to the attention of Daniel Custis, an intelligent and personable man twenty years older than she. Or perhaps it was at St. Peter's Church, which they both attended, or at one of the many social events the plantation society enjoyed. Since Custis lived only a few miles from Martha's home, their paths must have crossed many times. For years, Custis had seen Martha as nothing more than a pleasant child, a figure so familiar that he took her for granted. At seventeen, Martha Dandridge was grown up, and he could not take her for granted anymore.[6] What exactly caught his eye? An early biographer relies on portraits, descriptions, and a hint of imagination to give an intriguing picture:

> She was a charming girl, a little below medium stature, and possessed of an elegant figure. Her eyes were dark, and expressive of the most kindly good-nature, her complexion was fair, her hair a rich brown in color, her features were regular and beautiful, her whole face beamed with intelligence; she was sprightly and witty; and her manners were modest and extremely winning.[7]

Whether it was her youthful spirits, gentle manners, kindness, or witty conversation, Daniel Custis fell deeply in love. Martha returned his affection, and her father happily gave his blessing to the union. The only problem was Daniel's father, John Custis, an irritable and difficult man who had had a rocky relationship with his own wife before her death and wanted his son to marry a woman much richer than Martha.[8] Martha's father had only five hundred acres of land, whereas John Custis had seventeen thousand.[9] He angrily refused to consent to the wedding. In fact, he even gave away some of the family silver so Martha Dandridge would never be able to have it.

Daniel Custis was less fiery but just as stubborn as his father. Nothing was going to stop him from marrying Martha, but he wanted his father's blessing. While John Custis fumed, Daniel enlisted the aid of several friends to plead his cause. But it was Martha herself who finally won over her future father-in-law. In the spring of 1749, as Martha approached her eighteenth birthday, Daniel Custis received a remarkable letter from his friend, James Power:

> I am empowered by your father to let you know that he heartily and willingly consents to your marriage with Miss Dandridge; that he has so good a character of her that he rather you should have her than any lady in Virginia—nay, if possible, he is as much enamoured with her character as you are with her person, and this is owing chiefly to a prudent speech of her own.

The letter did not say where John Custis met Martha or what she said. It did, however, tell Daniel Custis exactly what to do. "Hurry down immediately for fear [your father] should change the strong inclination he has to your marrying directly."[10]

Shortly after reading the letter, Daniel Custis was off to Chestnut Grove, to share the good news and set a wedding date. But the eager groom's father did not live to see the wedding he had finally approved. On November 14, 1749, John Custis died, leaving a vast estate to his son. The couple waited almost six months after John Custis's death before getting married on May 15, 1750, at Chestnut Grove.[11]

A Historic Household

Archaeological digging in the Custis well has brought an array of historic objects to light. In addition to wine bottles, items excavated from the well include eighteenth-century drinking glasses, a silver shoe buckle, children's toys, flowerpots, and a gun barrel fashioned into a whistle. From such artifacts as these, archaeologists construct a picture of everyday life in the past.

Young Bride

Martha and her husband enjoyed a close and happy relationship. As mistress of the White House, the Custis plantation on the Pamunkey River, Martha Custis managed the domestic details of a much larger establishment than her father's. Daniel Custis's land covered six square miles. He had many slaves to work the fields and tend to his horses and cattle. With her doting husband, numerous friends, and elevated social position, the young matron lived an almost charmed existence.

In November 1751, Martha Custis gave birth to her first child, a little boy named Daniel Parke after his father. Two years later a daughter, Frances (Fanny), was born. Devoted and gentle, Martha Custis seemed made for motherhood. However, her happiness was shattered when Daniel Parke died at age three. His grieving mother became even more protective of Fanny and John Parke (Jacky), the son born in 1755.

The next year also brought changes to Martha Custis's family. In April 1756, her youngest sister, Mary, was born. Five months later, her father died. This pattern of happiness and sorrow coming almost hand in hand repeated itself often throughout Martha Custis's life. In 1757, she had another baby girl, Martha Parke (Patcy), but lost four-year-old Fanny. Some historians have suggested that grief for his children contributed to Daniel Custis's own decline in health. He died in July 1757.

Strong-minded Widow

Losing so many loved ones in a short space of time must have been devastating. But for all her gentleness, there was a core of steel to Martha Dandridge Custis. She had her religious faith and two small children to comfort her. "It gave me no small pleasure to hear with how great Christian patience and resignation you submitted to your late misfortune," wrote one of her husband's business associates. "The example is rare, though a duty incumbent upon us all." In a practical vein, the writer urged the young widow to assume administration of the Custis estate herself.[12]

Because her husband had died without a will, Martha Custis inherited one third of the estate, the remaining two thirds to be divided between her two children. Nothing in her experience had prepared her to conduct business, but she rose to the challenge. She completed an inventory and wrote to her London agents that transactions would continue as they had when her husband was alive. She also asked them to sell the tobacco she grew at the best possible price.

But Martha Custis may not have been as calm as she sounded. In cleaning out the Six Chimneys House in Williamsburg, where her father-in-law had lived, she threw many items down the well, including tea bowls, wine bottles, and fine drinking glasses.[13] Family heirlooms and other objects too valuable to throw away were auctioned off.[14] She even sold the family portraits. Perhaps this severe housecleaning allowed her to cope more easily with her grief.

Little is known of Martha Custis's life for the next few months. She lived quietly in her house on the Pamunkey, conducted business with the help of her husband's associates, and cherished her children. At the age of twenty-six, she was probably the wealthiest widow in Virginia.[15]

Chapter 3

ENTER A YOUNG
SOLDIER

Martha Custis was visiting her friends, the Chamberlaynes, at their plantation on the Pamunkey when a tall, impressive figure entered the room. Custis had probably met George Washington while her husband was still alive. Almost certainly they had friends in common and had come together at social occasions in Williamsburg. Since then, both their lives had changed greatly.[1] George Washington was the talk of Virginia.[2] Recently named colonel of the Virginia Regiment and commander in chief of all Virginia forces, he guarded the British boundaries in the Ohio Valley from the French and their Indian allies.

Almost at once Martha Custis and George Washington liked and respected each other.[3] Custis saw a tall man with a direct gaze, a thoughtful manner, and a pleasing gallantry.[4] But he looked alarmingly thin and pale after a recent bout of dysentery, a severe intestinal disorder and fever. Washington, in his turn, saw a short, softly curved woman of warmth and dignity—the ideal of the eighteenth-century lady.

A Brave Young Soldier

George Washington's legendary bravery and providential escapes were as apparent during the French and Indian War as they would be during the revolution. In one early battle near the Monongahela River, two horses were wounded and collapsed under him. Four bullets pierced his coat. One night, two groups of Washington's own men began firing on each other in confusion. Washington stopped them by riding into the middle of their battle and striking their guns with his sword.[5]

One week later, George Washington stopped at Custis's home on his way back from meetings with his doctor and the governor. Reassured about his health by one of the top physicians in the colony, George Washington felt much more optimistic about his future—and Martha Custis's. At twenty-six, he was more than ready to take a wife. Martha Custis, with her gentle ways and sensible outlook, seemed perfect for the role. Sometimes stiff and awkward in social situations, Washington felt relaxed and comfortable with Martha Custis. However, such a charming, rich woman was certain to attract many suitors. George Washington wasted little time in asking her to marry him.

Already Martha Custis had seen enough of the young commander to accept his proposal. She knew she needed a father for her children and a partner to care for her estate. Not only would Washington fill these roles honorably, but he would be a loyal, considerate companion—someone to make her happy again. Her period of grieving was over; it was time to look to the future.

But Martha Custis scarcely had a chance to get to know her future husband before he was off to fight for the British again. For six months, she anxiously awaited letters from her fiancé. Late in 1758, she heard Fort Duquesne in western Pennsylvania had been taken by Washington's men. The enemy had not even put up a fight. Although the French and Indian War was not over yet, Virginia's boundaries were safe for the time being. Washington felt that his part in the conflict was finished.[6] He resigned his commission and returned to Virginia.

Second Marriage

On January 6, 1759, surrounded by family and friends, George Washington and Martha Custis were married at the White House (later called Mount Vernon) by the Reverend David Mossum.[7]

Washington, in his white satin waistcoat with his dress sword at his side, towered over his plump, demure bride. At twenty-seven, Martha Custis was no longer young, but she looked lovely in her yellow brocade dress and high-heeled embroidered slippers. In the fashion of the day, her hair was powdered and entwined with pearls. After their honeymoon, the couple traveled to the Custis mansion in Williamsburg. George Washington had recently been elected to the state legislature. On February 22, his twenty-seventh birthday, he was sworn in as a burgess (representative) for Frederick County, Virginia.

New Home

Although they enjoyed the capital, the Washingtons planned to stay in Williamsburg only when the legislature was meeting. The young groom was eager to show his wife her new home in northern Virginia. That meant taking her farther away from her family and friends than she had ever been before.

In April 1759, several days of travel brought the carriage with Martha Washington, five-year-old Jacky, and three-year-old Patcy to Mount Vernon. A modest but well-cared-for home, it had been newly enlarged by George Washington in preparation for his marriage. Stepping through the central hallway, Martha Washington found herself looking down a gentle hillside to a breathtaking, panoramic view of the Potomac River. Indoors, she found the furniture and staircase well polished and the beds freshly made in accordance with the orders her husband had sent ahead the previous day. It was time to settle in and put her own stamp on Mount Vernon.

Soon Mrs. Washington was busy doing what she did best—supervising domestic details and entertaining guests. One of the first people she met was Sally Fairfax, wife of George William Fairfax of the nearby plantation, Belvoir. Sally Fairfax

Life on the Plantation

Virginia plantations in the mid-eighteenth century were almost like self-sufficient little kingdoms. Although luxuries had to be imported from London, the plantations were well equipped to produce necessities like food and cloth. Slaves were skilled at making such items as shoes, wheels, iron goods, candles, and soap.[8]

was a witty, outspoken, and beautiful woman with whom George Washington had once believed himself in love. Whatever Martha Washington guessed about her husband's feelings, she welcomed Sally Fairfax to her home as graciously as she did everyone else. The two women became close friends.[9] Already Martha Washington understood the depth of her husband's loyalty and his deep attachment to her.[10] She trusted him in almost everything.

Only where her children were concerned did Martha Washington insist on her own way. She was a protective and doting mother. Occasionally, she spoiled her children. George Washington himself was a conscientious stepparent, attentive and kind. He always called Jacky and Patcy "the children," never "my wife's children," and he did everything possible to promote their well-being.[11]

Luxuries from England

Martha and George Washington wanted a gracious lifestyle for the children as well as for themselves. Since colonial industries were not allowed to compete with English goods, many items were not available locally. Washington sent long, detailed orders to his agent in London. From bedspreads and curtains to fire screens, parlor ornaments, shoes, and toys, he described exactly what he wanted.

Martha Washington, who enjoyed wearing beautiful clothes, looked forward to the stylish silks and kid gloves she received. She wore her fine clothes whenever she accompanied her husband to Williamsburg. But she had little use for fashion as she went about her daily chores. "Neat—but not gaudy," was how she described her taste in clothes.[12]

Plantation Mistress

Like her husband, Martha Washington was an early riser. Before breakfast she gave instructions to her cook and housekeeper. Right after the morning meal she retired to her room for an hour of religious devotion and quiet contemplation. She was so strict about this practice that not even Jacky and Patcy were allowed to disturb her. Perhaps this private hour was what enabled her to be continuously active the rest of the day. She bustled back and forth between the spinning house, the wash house, and the mansion. She was constantly watching the children, entertaining neighbors, or teaching servants to knit and sew. One hundred fifty slaves had come to Mount Vernon from the Custis estate. Their needs and physical well-being occupied a good portion of Martha Washington's day.

So did food preparation. One observer noted that Martha Washington "inspected everything daily, giving out with her own hands the meals, going into the dairy, the cellar. . . ."[13] Every evening she personally supervised the bread making. In the small, thick-walled smokehouse, she took special care with the curing of her meats. "Virginia ladies value themselves on the goodness of their bacon," George Washington once explained.[14]

Scarcely a day went by without guests coming to Mount Vernon. George Washington carefully noted all visitors in his diary. These included the governors of Maryland and Virginia and other important people. In a seven-year period, about two thousand guests dined with the Washingtons.[15] Sometimes during the hunting season, they invited people to stay with them for several weeks. There was nothing George Washington enjoyed better than a good fox hunt with friends. Martha Washington served the hunters satisfying meals afterward.

Early in the marriage, George Washington had written, "I am now, I beleive fixd at this Seat with an agreable Consort for Life and hope to find more happiness in retirement than I ever experiencd amidst a wide and bustling world."[16] Surely his wife agreed that her life was nearly perfect. The only thing she could have asked for was another child. But Martha and George Washington would never have children of their own.

Jacky and Patcy continued to be the center of Martha Washington's life.[17] In an era of high childhood death rates, she worried about them constantly. In 1762, she wrote to her sister about a trip she had taken without her son: "I was quite impatiant to get home if I at any time heard the doggs barke or a noise out I thought thair was a person sent for me I often fansied he was sick or some accident had happened to him . . ."[18]

Preoccupied with her husband and children, Martha Washington kept busy from morning to night. It did not seem possible that anything could change in her happy, well-ordered existence. But political decisions brewing in Great Britain were soon to threaten her private world and the peace of all thirteen American colonies.

Chapter 4

TROUBLE ON THE HORIZON

T axation without representation was a phrase Martha Washington heard more and more often in the mid-1760s. The reason for the taxes seemed simple enough. In 1763, the French and Indian War had finally ended with England's gaining almost all the land in North America that had belonged to the French. But winning the war had cost a vast amount of money, and the English Parliament (legislature) thought the colonies should help pay future costs. In 1765, Parliament passed the Stamp Act, which imposed taxes on almost everything printed in the colonies. Whether it was for a newspaper, property deed, a marriage license, or simply a deck of playing cards, colonists would be required to buy a special stamp. Many Americans resented this measure because they could not vote for or against the tax. Since Americans were not represented in

Parliament, should that distant body be allowed to exert such control over them? Taxation without representation became a rallying cry for those who opposed England's meddling in the colonies' affairs.

Suspicion of Treason

As a member of the Virginia House of Burgesses, George Washington had many opportunities to discuss the situation. However, he left the state capital before the spring legislative session of 1765 ended. It was not until afterward that a neighbor who had been present in Williamsburg told the Washingtons of a fiery speech made by Patrick Henry. Calling the Stamp Act tyranny, Henry refused to back down when the speaker of the House referred to his remarks as treason, an action disloyal to the government. "And if this be treason, make the most of it!" Henry retorted, shocking and inspiring his listeners.[1] His five resolutions against the Stamp Act narrowly passed.

Treason! The word was startling and alarming. Surely a simple tax dispute did not call for such a drastic response. Martha Washington listened as her husband discussed the situation over and over. Although the Stamp Act displeased him greatly, she could hardly imagine his committing treason.[2]

George Washington did approve a ban on all colonial business requiring the stamps. But before that became a big inconvenience, the Stamp Act was revoked. Relieved, Martha Washington traveled south that November with her husband and children. She was happy to stay at her sister's home in the small town of Eltham, Virginia, while her husband proceeded to Williamsburg for the legislative session. The capital was close enough for Martha Washington to slip into town occasionally for a play, a ball, or dinner at the governor's palace. There was so much to think about besides stamps and taxes.

But Parliament was still determined to make the colonists share the cost of any future wars. The very next year it passed the Townshend Acts, which created an import tax on articles such as ink, paint, paper, glass, and tea. Again, George Washington became involved in lengthy discussions about what Americans could do to assert their rights.

Patcy Custis's Illness

Martha Washington had another concern that struck even closer to home. On June 14, 1768, her twelve-year-old daughter Patcy had a seizure. "Sent for Doctr. Rumney to Patcy Custis who was seized with fitts," reads George Washington's diary entry for that date.[3] Very little was known about "falling sickness," as epilepsy was often called then. Baffled and terrified, Martha Washington knew only that Patcy sometimes lost control of herself and seemed unaware of her surroundings. There was no telling when the next seizure would occur. "We set out to go to Captn. McCarty's," George Washington wrote in his journal, "but Patcy being taken with a fit on the road by the Mill, we turnd back."[4] Every kind of medicine was tried, but Patcy did not get better. Martha went about her household chores with a heavy heart.

While she anxiously watched over Patcy, Martha Washington also worried about Jacky, who went away to school for the first time the year his sister became ill. Was he happy? Was he well? Did he miss home? The growing tension with England may have added to his mother's uneasiness but could hardly have outweighed her concern for her children.

Protesting the Townshend Acts

Meanwhile, anger against the Townshend Acts was mounting. George Washington was deeply upset about the situation and anxious to end Parliament's unwelcome meddling. Like his neighbor and fellow legislator, George Mason, Washington believed a boycott was the answer. Mason had written a list of English items that he believed Virginians should refuse to purchase. Foodstuffs and wine were no real problem. The colonies could easily supply their own needs in those areas. However, there were other items that would represent a real sacrifice to lovers of comfort and elegance like George and Martha Washington. Mason wanted to end the import of jewelry, watches, clocks, mirrors, cabinets, carriages, many fabrics, and shoes. Many of these items could not be easily duplicated in Virginia.

The Boston Massacre

On March 5, 1770, a mob of angry Americans began heckling the British guard at the Boston Customs House. His cries for help brought a small group of British soldiers to the rescue. Violence erupted, and five Americans died in what came to be called the Boston Massacre. One of the victims was a runaway slave named Crispus Attucks. His courage and patriotism earned him the title "first martyr of the American Revolution."[5]

George Washington felt the boycott would send a strong message that the English Parliament would not be able to ignore. But he was already thinking of ways to go beyond the boycott if necessary. He wrote to Mason:

> At a time when our lordly Masters in Great Britain will be satisfied with nothing less than the deprication [insult] of American freedom, it seems highly necessary that something should be done to avert the stroke and maintain the liberty which we have derived from our ancestors. . . . That no man should scruple, or hesitate a moment to use a[r]ms in defence of so valuable a blessing . . . is clearly my opinion.[6]

George Washington was not one to use words lightly or to make idle threats. When Mason's proposal was adopted that spring, Martha Washington braced herself to do without the many small luxuries she had always welcomed from England. Any sacrifice, even if it involved her family's comfort, must have seemed better than armed conflict.

Chapter 5

SPARTAN MOTHER

O nce again, England backed down. In 1770, Parliament revoked the Townshend Acts, though the tax on tea remained. Many merchants began trading with England again. Even George Washington resumed placing orders for English goods. But even having luxuries again could do little to allay Martha Washington's anxiety for her daughter Patcy.

A Mother's Fears

When Patcy was well, Martha Washington watched her beautiful daughter receive visitors, practice the piano, and attend dancing classes and balls. It was an upbringing similar to her own. But however healthy and happy Patcy seemed at times, she continued to suffer seizures. For a short time in 1770, George Washington kept a record of her illness. On twenty-six out of eighty-six days, Patcy suffered from "fits." Sometimes she had two a day.[1] In her heart, Martha Washington wondered if her daughter would ever be able to live a normal life.

Meanwhile, George Washington wondered whether Jacky would ever do well in his studies. To his stepfather's distress, Jacky knew little Latin, Greek, or even plain arithmetic. A friendly, easygoing young man, he preferred socializing to studying.

Martha Washington let her husband do most of the worrying about Jacky's education. She knew her son was loyal, gallant, and charming—a trifle spoiled, a bit lazy, but what was that compared to a kind heart? Whenever Jacky returned home, his mother rejoiced. In May 1772, Jacky arrived, accompanied by an artist named Charles Willson Peale. Eagerly, Martha Washington grabbed the chance to have the members of her family painted by a professional artist.

When George Washington put on his old military uniform to pose for Peale, he could not know how soon he would be wearing it for a different reason. Relations with England were relatively smooth in 1772. The Virginia Assembly, which had been dismissed by the governor several years ago, was meeting regularly again. Now the colony had a new royal governor, John Murray, the earl of Dunmore. George Washington dined with him that November when the family returned to Williamsburg. As usual, Martha Washington spent time at her sister's home in Eltham, but on November 12, she accompanied her husband to a ball. At age forty-one, she had given up dancing, but she still loved good conversation and music.

A Surprise Engagement

George Washington continued to worry about Jacky's studies. He was considering a new school for his stepson when the eighteen-year-old declared that he was engaged to be married.

This created a new headache for George Washington, who considered Jacky Custis too young and immature to be married. The Washingtons had met Eleanor (Nelly) Calvert while visiting Jacky at school in Annapolis. They found her lovely and personable, but she was not quite sixteen. Age did not seem as great a barrier to Martha Washington as to her husband, however.[2]

After all, she had first married at age eighteen and had always been more concerned with Jacky's happiness than with his sense of responsibility. Still, she agreed with her husband that it would be a good idea for the young couple to wait.

Nelly's father, Benedict Calvert, also agreed that the couple should postpone their wedding. In May 1773, George Washington took his stepson to his new school, King's College in New York, which later became Columbia University. After seeing Jacky comfortably settled, George Washington returned to Mount Vernon.

A Tragedy and a Wedding

It was a crowded, happy dinner table that Martha Washington hosted on June 19, 1773. Nelly Calvert and her friends had come to visit, and George Washington's brother's family added to the general cheer. Most important to her mother, Patcy Custis appeared well and happy. However, soon after the seventeen-year-old left the table, she suffered a seizure. There was nothing anyone could do for her. Within two minutes, Patcy Custis was dead. She died, wrote George Washington, "without uttering a word or scarce a sigh. This sudden and unexpected blow, I scarce need add has almost reduced my poor wife to the lowest ebb of misery."[3]

After the funeral, George Washington devoted himself to his wife. He tried to help her forget her sorrow, if only briefly, by taking her on outings to nearby plantations.[4]

In her grief, Martha Washington missed her son more than ever. In fact, her longing for Jacky may have been what prompted her husband to remove the young man from school in late 1773 and give his consent to a speedy wedding.

On February 3, 1774, George Washington set out with Lund Washington, his cousin and property manager, to Nelly's home in Maryland, where Jacky was to be married that evening. Still mourning, the mother of the groom remained at home, but tradition says that she sent a letter to Nelly to welcome her to the family.

Political Excitement in Williamsburg

Several months after Jacky's wedding, Martha Washington felt ready to accompany her husband to Williamsburg.[5] Perhaps she simply needed his presence at a time when she missed Patcy so deeply. Or perhaps she felt it her duty to take her place at his side. Whatever her reasons, on May 12, 1774, George and Martha Washington set off to attend to political affairs in the capital.

Williamsburg was seething with excitement. One year earlier, in 1773, Parliament had passed the Tea Act, which gave great business advantages to the British East India Company. The law enabled the company to sell tea so cheaply that other merchants could not compete. Even smugglers could not sell tea for such a low price. Once again, the colonies were enraged by England's interference in their affairs. Angry citizens in New York and Philadelphia managed to stop the company's ships from landing there. However, ships bearing cargoes of tea did land in Boston, Massachusetts. On December 16, 1773, a group of determined patriots threw 342 chests of tea into the water in order to avoid paying the tax on the tea when it was unloaded from the ships.[6]

By the time the Washingtons arrived in Williamsburg the following May, Parliament had decided to close the port of Boston in retaliation for what would become known as the Boston Tea Party. This extreme measure meant that no ships would be allowed to enter or leave the harbor. All trade would cease, and no supplies could arrive by sea.

Martha Washington took great interest in this newest dispute with the mother country, as England was called.[7] Caught up in the rapidly moving events, she could hardly do otherwise. Within a week of her arrival in Williamsburg, the General Assembly declared a day of fasting and prayer on the date that the port of Boston was to close. But before this symbolic gesture took place, Virginia Governor Dunmore disbanded the House of Burgesses for what he called disloyalty to England. Undaunted, the legislators left the courthouse and continued to meet at the Raleigh Tavern.

Political differences were one thing; manners and hospitality were another. The same evening that the House of Burgesses was dismissed, George Washington attended a dinner at the governor's palace. The next day, Martha joined her husband for a ball in honor of the governor's wife and children, newly arrived from New York. However, no ball would keep the Washingtons from observing the appointed day of sympathy with Boston.

Burning Question

That summer at Mount Vernon, Martha Washington enjoyed a visit from Nelly Custis, her new daughter-in-law. Meanwhile, her husband and son returned to Williamsburg for a special convention. The pair arrived home with the news that George Washington was a delegate to the First Continental Congress, which would be held in September in Philadelphia. Representatives from all the colonies were invited to discuss England's latest tyranny. A burning question loomed in everyone's mind: How should the other colonies react to the closing of the port of Boston in Massachusetts?

Brave Farewell

The night before his departure, Martha Washington planned an elegant meal for her husband and his guests: Patrick Henry, Edmund Pendleton, and George Mason. The first two men, also delegates to Congress, would accompany George Washington to Philadelphia. One biographer has suggested that this dinner party may have been the first time Martha Washington heard a statement her husband had made at the recent convention. George Washington had vowed: "I will raise one thousand men, subsist them at my own expense, and march myself at their head for the relief of Boston."[8]

These were shocking words. Martha Washington must have felt nervous about her husband's strong declaration and about the Congress in general.[9] If a governor could dismiss the colonial assembly simply for fasting and praying, what might be the retaliation for holding such a meeting? Despite her misgivings, she spoke cheerfully and confidently to the men gathered at her table. "I hope you will all stand firm," she declared. "I know George will."[10]

Edmund Pendleton was impressed. Martha Washington reminded him of the war-time bravery of ancient Greek women. "[She] talked like a Spartan to her son on his going to battle," he later wrote.[11] As the trio set off in the morning, Martha Washington waved from the doorway. "God be with you, gentlemen!" she called.[12]

It was late October when Martha Washington welcomed her husband home again. Immediately she sensed his somber mood. Not only had the Congress taken new measures to enforce a boycott against English imports, it had rechanneled taxes from the official treasury to itself. It had encouraged town militias to gather arms and prepare for possible conflict. George Washington showed his support by drilling a company of young men in Alexandria, Virginia, urging his fellow Virginians to raise troops. War was coming, and the colonists had to be ready.[13]

The First Battle

The first major battle of the revolution took place just about the time Washington was selected commander in chief. Trying to dislodge the Americans from their strong position atop Breed's Hill in Boston, the British were driven back twice. Although the Americans' ammunition finally ran out and they were forced to retreat, it was a hollow conquest for the British. Almost half their troops had been killed or wounded. British General Sir Henry Clinton called it "A dear bought victory—another such would have ruined us."[14]

The Shot Heard Round the World

Over the next few months, George Washington's prediction of violence began to come true. In accordance with resolves of the Continental Congress, the town of Concord, Massachusetts, had begun to collect weapons. Governor Thomas Gage of Massachusetts felt this was going much too far and sent soldiers to destroy the colonists' arsenal. On April 19, 1775, these British troops were challenged by a group of American militiamen at Lexington, Massachusetts. Someone fired a gun, and a small skirmish ensued. The British soldiers marched through the colony to Concord, where more shots were exchanged. The Revolutionary War had begun with results that would be heard around the world.

The Unpaid General

By his own direction, George Washington received no salary as commander in chief of the American forces. He only asked to be paid for his expenses.[15]

Commander in Chief

When George Washington left for Philadelphia to attend the Second Continental Congress in May 1775, he wore his military uniform, which must have been an ominous sign to his wife. His letters did little to reassure her. George Washington gave no indication of when he might return home. Perhaps this omission warned Martha Washington that her husband was being tapped for a tremendous burden, honor, and responsibility. But even if she had anticipated her husband's new role, Martha Washington still must have been stunned by his letter of June 18, 1775. George Washington wrote: "It has been determined in Congress, that the whole Army raised for the defence of the American Cause shall be put under my care, and that it is necessary for me to proceed immediately to Boston . . ."[16] Her husband had been selected to be commander in chief of all American forces. He was not coming home after all. His next words were sweet but could hardly have softened the blow:

> You may believe me my dear Patcy, when I assure you, in the most solemn manner, that, so far from seeking this appointment I have used every endeavour in my power to avoid it, not only from my unwillingness to part with you and the Family, but from a consciousness of its being a trust too great for my Capacity and that I should enjoy more real happiness and felicity in one month with you, at home, than I have the most distant prospect of reaping abroad, if my stay was to be Seven times Seven years.[17]

With her husband gone and no children at home, Martha Washington had little prospect of happiness, either.

Chapter 6

INDEPENDENCE

Although she was invited to visit her sister near Williamsburg, Martha Washington felt her place was at Mount Vernon that summer of 1775. She expected to see her husband in the fall and hoped the additions already begun on their home would be finished by then. Diligently, she supervised work on her husband's new study and their new bedroom. But even though Martha Washington kept busy, she found waiting hard. She told Lund Washington that if only the general would agree, she would happily travel to Boston to be with him.[1]

The anxious wife got her wish when a letter arrived from the general, asking her to join him in Cambridge, Massachusetts. Martha Washington was overjoyed and perhaps a little overwhelmed. She had never been so far from home in her life.

In spite of the cold weather and short notice, she was soon ready to leave with her son and daughter-in-law. Countless American patriots greeted her on her passage north. Each rousing welcome deepened Martha Washington's gratitude and realization of the public role she now had to play.[2]

Arrival at Headquarters

On December 11, 1775, Martha Washington's carriage rolled up to the general's headquarters in Cambridge, Massachusetts. After almost six months of waiting, she was about to see her husband again.

Headquarters became a happier, more sociable place as Martha Washington settled in. With her quiet tact and gentle warmth, she easily made visitors feel at home.

The Washingtons celebrated Christmas surrounded by guests. Just before the New Year, Martha Washington wrote to a friend of her contentment and fears:

> *Every person seems to be cheerfull and happy hear,—some days we have a number of cannon and shells from Boston and Bunkers hill, but it does not seem to surprise anyone but me; I confess I shudder every time I hear the sound of a gun— . . . Charlestown has only a few chimneys standing in it . . . they are pulling up all the wharfs for firewood—to me that never see any thing of war, the preparations are very terable indeed, but I endever to keep my fears to myself as well as I can.[3]*

Phillis Wheatley

In March 1776, George Washington met with a remarkable African-American woman named Phillis Wheatley. Kidnapped and brought to the colonies as a slave in 1761, she was purchased by John Wheatley as a servant for his wife. However, Phillis Wheatley was treated more like a member of the family and studied Greek and Latin with Mrs. Wheatley and her daughters. These were considerable accomplishments for any woman, but it was her poetry that made Wheatley a celebrity in New England. In 1775, about two years after she became free, Wheatley sent George Washington a poem she had written about him, which led to their subsequent meeting.[4]

As spring advanced with the threat of more fighting, Martha Washington and other women rolled bandages and stitched clothing in her small parlor.[5] The occasional boom of a distant cannon reminded them to hurry. Something was about to happen.

Overnight Victory

One night in early March, the American troops used cannons, recently obtained from a British fort in New York, to fortify the hills overlooking Boston. When British troops arose on March 5, 1776, they were shocked to find themselves surrounded by American artillery. Five days later, the British evacuated the city. Boston once again belonged to the Americans.

Shortly after the American troops took Boston, Martha Washington invited her new friend Mercy Warren to accompany her into the city. The two women set out early in the morning. Crossing the Charles River from Cambridge, they discovered a desolate scene. Buildings had been demolished for firewood; stores had been sacked and food left to rot in the streets. Salt and spoiled molasses caked the roadsides. Martha Washington was deeply saddened. How many other cities would suffer before the war was over?

Army on the Move

Now that the British had left Boston, George Washington moved his headquarters to New York. Although he had a comfortable house and a splendid view of the Hudson River, headquarters was a much tenser place than it had been in Boston. The general was constantly on the go between his residence and a smaller office in the city. Martha Washington knew he worried about the difficulty of defending New York against the British ships expected to arrive. His problems were further complicated by the unwelcome news that paid German troops called Hessians would be joining the British in America.

Fighting Smallpox

Another worry plagued the Washingtons. Smallpox was taking a fierce toll among the American soldiers. General Washington believed inoculations could help stop the sometimes fatal disease. In addition to his worries about the soldiers' health, George Washington was deeply concerned about his wife. He wanted her to be inoculated, too.

Although many people feared inoculation and the mild case of smallpox it induced, Martha Washington decided to risk it. In May, she went with her husband to Philadelphia to be inoculated. Two weeks later, the general reported to his brother-in-law at

An Early Feminist

Mercy Otis Warren believed that women were as intellectually capable as men. Not content with the traditional role of women, this early feminist wrote poems, plays, and history. She knew most of the colonial leaders, and in 1812, she published a three-volume history of the American Revolution.[6]

Eltham that she was "now in the Small Pox by Innoculation and like to have it very favorably having got through the Fever and not more than about a dozen Pustules appearing (this being the 13th day since the Infection was received)."[7]

July 4, 1776

Martha Washington had returned to New York by the time British ships were seen approaching the harbor in late June. For her own safety, the general sent her back to Philadelphia. She was still in the city on July 4, 1776, when the bell in the State House began to peal loudly. The sudden clamor announced that the Declaration of Independence had been adopted by the Continental Congress. The last chance of compromise with England was over. Her husband was now fighting for a new and free America.

Four days later, a crowd gathered around the great hall to hear the document read. Cheers erupted as Thomas Jefferson's stirring words rang through the square, proclaiming that "these United Colonies are, and of right ought to be, free and independent States."[8]

American Retreat

Martha Washington's spirits hovered between patriotism and anxiety as she waited for news from New York. Soon she learned that learned that her husband's forces had been defeated by the British on Long Island. Fatigued and discouraged, many Americans had deserted the army. The day after his troops retreated across the East River, the general wrote, "For the forty-eight hours preceding [the crossing] I had hardly been off my horse and had never closed my eyes . . ."[9]

The next news Martha Washington received was equally bleak. The British had landed at Kip's Bay just north of New York City and sent the Americans fleeing. Her husband was safe, but the stories that swept through Philadelphia terrified Martha Washington. The angry general had ridden after his retreating troops, rallying them to battle. Finally, he gathered several hundred men together. But when a band of sixty or seventy British soldiers headed their way, the American soldiers scattered in all directions. Unprotected as his men fled, the general and his aides were forced to retreat. George Washington seethed over the disgrace.[10]

Martha Washington agonized over such tidings, too. Suddenly, the familiarity of home seemed more comforting than being close

Declaring Independence

The American colonies became a new nation on July 2, 1776, when the Continental Congress passed Richard Henry Lee's resolutions calling for separation from England. Two days later, "The Unanimous Declaration of the 13 United States of America" was formally approved. Later this would become known as the Declaration of Independence. Contrary to popular belief, no one actually signed the document until August 2.[11]

to the action.[12] There was another reason for Martha Washington to leave Philadelphia. Nelly and Jacky Custis had just had a baby. At Mount Airy, Maryland, she saw her granddaughter Eliza Parke Custis for the first time. Momentarily forgetting the war, Martha Washington joyfully welcomed the newest addition to her family.

Chapter 7

VICTORY AND SORROW

Martha Washington had established a pattern that would last the rest of the Revolutionary War. Every winter when fighting stopped, she joined her husband at headquarters. Every spring, when fighting resumed, she returned to Mount Vernon. After spending early 1777 at Morristown, she experienced an anxious fall waiting for news. The British had marched into Philadelphia, and a dense fog had hindered the Americans when they tried to force the British out of nearby Germantown.

Sometimes it seemed as if Martha Washington's personal fortunes wavered almost as much as the war. In December 1777, her second grandchild and namesake, little Martha, was born. Then before Christmas, her sister Nancy Bassett died. Even though Jacky Custis brought his wife and babies to comfort her, Martha Washington had a difficult Christmas as she mourned her sister and worried about her husband.

Valley Forge

It was mid-January before Martha Washington received word that she could join her husband at Valley Forge. Several weeks later, her carriage swayed between rows of small, primitive huts on the road to headquarters. Haggard soldiers, numb with cold, watched the coach pass. Some raised frostbitten hands, bound in tattered strips of cloth, to wave. Many men had also wrapped their feet in rags for warmth. But if Martha Washington had looked carefully in the gathering twilight, she could have seen trails of blood left in the snow by barefoot soldiers.

As always, Martha Washington turned her attention to the hungry, suffering men. A local woman recalled her efforts: "Every fair day she might be seen, with basket in hand, and with a single attendant, going among the huts seeking the keenest and most needy sufferers, and giving all the comfort in her power." She also knit socks, made shirts, and mended old clothes.[1] After delivering a nourishing meal to one dying soldier, she was overcome with grief and pity. Kneeling down by the man's straw pallet, she prayed out loud for him and for his wife.

Cries of "God bless Lady Washington" often greeted Martha Washington as she trudged from hut to hut, bringing relief to the men.[2] But no matter how much she did, much more remained to be done.

The general continued to ask Congress for supplies while his men ransacked the countryside for food. At last Congress came through with the desperately needed provisions. The men felt better physically, but they still had a lot to learn about being soldiers. A Prussian volunteer, Baron Friedrich von Steuben, soon arrived to help drill them. He taught the men to march in formation and to use bayonets. He trained them in different fighting techniques. Responding to his demands, the soldiers took pride in their accomplishments.

Help from France

Welcome news arrived at the beginning of May. France, England's old enemy, had officially recognized the United States as an independent country. Soon the Americans could expect valuable military aid from the French. On May 6, 1778, the troops celebrated with an enormous picnic and a parade. Martha

Washington and the other officers' wives watched the precision with which the men arranged themselves on the field for the *feu de joie* (the fire of joy, a ceremonial firing of cannons and muskets). Thanks to Baron von Steuben, the Americans were no longer a mismatched assembly of awkward young men. They were a real army.

Perhaps the memory of the splendid review comforted Martha Washington that summer as she waited at Mount Vernon. Shortly after she left Valley Forge, the British evacuated Philadelphia and headed for New York. Foreseeing this move, Washington attacked them en route at Monmouth Courthouse in Pennsylvania. When American Major General Charles Lee started to retreat, a furious Washington, oblivious to personal danger, rode his horse all over the field, gathering soldiers for the fight. The men responded to his courageous example and held their position. Although the general had hoped to pursue the British the day after the battle, the enemy troops disappeared during the night. Because they had a head start and his own troops were so worn out, Washington decided not to follow them after all.[3]

Second Winter at Morristown

Martha Washington spent the winter of 1779 at headquarters in Middletown, New Jersey. She found the soldiers healthier and better sheltered than she remembered. But the next fall, when she returned to the second encampment at Morristown, New Jersey, she endured her worst winter yet. Blizzards dumped up to six feet of snow at a time. The soldiers, cramped in small, primitive huts, lacked warm clothes and nourishing food. Martha Washington tried to identify the neediest individuals and bring them food and blankets. But she could never do enough to relieve the men's suffering. Perhaps that is why when soldiers broke

The War Comes to Mount Vernon

In 1781, British soldiers appeared at Mount Vernon. In George and Martha Washington's absence, their manager, Lund Washington, offered the enemy troops refreshments and allowed them to take several slaves. George Washington was deeply chagrined and anxious for the well-being of the missing slaves. He wrote to Lund Washington: "It would have been a less painful circumstance to have heard that in consequence of your noncompliance with their request they had burnt my house and laid my plantation in ruins."[4]

army rules, she asked her husband to excuse the culprits. Her friendship and charity made the terrible winter a little more bearable for the soldiers.

The spring brought both good news and bad. The Marquis de Lafayette, a young Frenchman who had volunteered his services in the American Army, returned from a trip to France with the promise of six fighting ships and six thousand French soldiers. However, a story in the *New York Gazette* told of the surrender of Charleston, South Carolina, to the British. It was time for Martha Washington to return home.

Sustained by her daily chores at Mount Vernon, Martha Washington waited anxiously for news. She rejoiced when French troops arrived in July and agonized when the British defeated the Americans at Camden, South Carolina, in August. Martha Washington could only imagine what her husband must be feeling. What would happen to their lives if the British won the war? That winter of 1780–1781 she joined him again at New Windsor, New York, on the Hudson River. With her husband, she grieved over news of mutiny among the underfed and underpaid troops in New Jersey and Pennsylvania.[5] Sadly she returned home the following June, stopping on the way to see friends in Philadelphia.

George Washington En Route to Yorktown

The American situation looked desperate. British General Cornwallis had advanced into Williamsburg, causing the Virginia General Assembly to flee to Richmond. Then Martha Washington received the startling news that her husband was heading south to confront Cornwallis at Yorktown, Virginia. En route, he would stop briefly at Mount Vernon—his first trip home in six years.

Joy and anxiety fluttered in her heart as Martha Washington thought of the reunion—and the battle. For a few days, Mount Vernon was more like army headquarters than her peaceful home. Martha Washington did everything possible to make her husband's aides comfortable at the same time she welcomed her son Jacky and his family. The Custises had come to greet the general and let him meet their four children.

Jacky Custis shared his parents' hope, determination, and patriotism. He became so excited about the approaching conflict that he decided to accompany the soldiers to Yorktown. Martha Washington's brief respite was over. On September 12, 1781, she sent both her husband and her son off to battle.

Deciding Battle

The waiting must have seemed endless to Martha Washington as she mentally followed the soldiers on their march and wondered how they were doing. By September 28, General Washington's and French General Jean Comte de Rochambeau's troops were within sight of Yorktown. As the British watched uneasily, the American and French troops began digging shelters and preparing for the attack. On October 9, 1781, George Washington fired the first cannon, officially beginning the battle.[6] The bombardment continued for days, and the British suffered heavy losses. Their food supplies were running low, and they were cut off from all means of escape by French warships. Eight days after the siege began, General Cornwallis was forced to surrender.

Although neither side knew it at the time, the British defeat marked an approaching end to the war. The fighting was not completely over, but it would soon be time to discuss peace.

No Chance to Rejoice

For Martha Washington, there was no relief. Almost as soon as tidings of the American victory reached her, she learned that her son had camp fever, a dangerous illness that caused a high fever and intestinal distress. Panic-stricken, Martha Washington set out at once with Jacky's wife, Nelly, and five-year-old daughter,

Eliza, to see him. The general joined them at Jacky's bedside just before the young man died on November 5, 1781. Martha Washington had outlived all her children.

Though heartbroken, the stricken mother put on a brave front. She had her religious faith, her husband, and four grandchildren to comfort her. She also had the memory of a son who cared so much for his country that even when he was dying, he arranged to watch the British surrender. After the funeral at Eltham, she returned to Mount Vernon with her husband and her son's widow and daughter. One week later, when General Washington left for Philadelphia, his wife was at his side.

An End to Fighting

By 1783, everyone knew the war was over. Congress had ratified the peace treaty with England on April 15. Three days later, George Washington declared an end to combat. But fighting or no fighting, the army needed a commander in chief until the treaty was signed by the American diplomats in France. That meant another delay as the treaty crossed and recrossed the ocean. General Washington wrote of his longing for "that relaxation and repose which is absolutely necessary to me."[7]

It was necessary to his wife, too. In early October, Martha Washington, followed by six wagons full of furniture and documents, left Rocky Hill, near Princeton, New Jersey. She wanted to reach Mount Vernon before winter snow made the roads treacherous.[8] Surely, this year the general would be home for Christmas, and there was much to do to get ready.

Peace Treaty

When Martha Washington left, she could not know that the peace treaty had already been signed on September 3. Word of the signing did not reach Princeton for nearly two months. In

December, General Washington said a heartfelt good-bye to his officers and proceeded to Annapolis, Maryland, where Congress was then meeting.

Martha Washington, who was later to boast that she had heard the opening and closing shots of the revolution probably came to see her husband resign his commission.[9] Seated in the gallery, she watched her husband enter the Senate chamber of Maryland's state capitol on December 23, 1783. "Having now finished the work assigned me, I retire from the great theatre of action," Washington announced.[10]

Agreements for Peace

Peace talks to end the Revolutionary War were held in France and attended by Benjamin Franklin, John Adams, and John Jay. In the Treaty of Paris, England recognized American independence and gave the new country all the land between the Allegheny Mountains and the Mississippi River. This doubled the size of the original thirteen colonies. The United States promised to end persecution of Loyalists (those who remained loyal to England) and to return the land that had been seized from them.[11]

George and Martha Washington arrived at Mount Vernon on Christmas Eve, 1783. Soon they were surrounded by Nelly's children, eager to welcome their grandparents home. Looking around at the happy faces of her loved ones, Martha Washington knew the war was truly over at last.

Chapter 8

GOD BLESS LADY WASHINGTON

Throughout the holidays, Martha Washington fondly cared for her grandchildren. With her son gone, she felt a deep need to have children around her always. Jacky's widow, Nelly, who had recently remarried, agreed to let the Washingtons unofficially adopt her two youngest children, five-year-old Eleanor Parke Custis (Nelly) and three-year-old George Washington Parke Custis (called Wash and, occasionally, Tub). The two older girls, Eliza and Martha (nicknamed Patcy as her grandmother and aunt had been) often visited Mount Vernon, too.

Well-resorted Tavern

Surrounded by the younger generation, Martha Washington continued her household routine and entertained the many guests who came to visit the general. Not only diplomats and soldiers, but also businessmen, inventors, artists, and ministers came to call. "A well resorted tavern," George Washington humorously described Mount Vernon, "as scarcely any travelers who are going from north to south or south to north do not spend a day or two in it."[1] In fact, so many people flocked to Mount Vernon that one evening when the Washingtons dined alone, the general considered it a circumstance unusual enough to be noted in his diary.[2]

Now in her fifties, Martha Washington was hearty, stout, gray-haired, and cheerful. "Of good complexion," one visitor described her, "has a large portly double chin and an open and engaging Countenance [face], on which a pleasing smile sets during conversation, in which she bears an agreeable part."[3] Often the talk centered around the recent war. "It is astonishing," another visitor reported, "with what raptures Mrs. Washington spoke about the discipline of the army, the excellent order they were in . . . What pleasure she took in the sound of the fifes an drums preferring it to any music that was ever heard."[4]

Though she fondly remembered the young soldiers, Martha Washington believed her days of adventure were behind her. The greatest challenges she expected to face were domestic—like planning her niece Fanny's wedding at Mount Vernon or spreading a plentiful table after the dog ran off with the ham she had planned to serve for dinner. She discussed decorations for the grand ballroom that had been added to Mount Vernon during her husband's absence. But larger issues rarely concerned her. "We have not a single article of news but pollitick which I do not concern myself with," she wrote.[5]

Constitutional Convention

In May 1787, when George Washington left home to attend the Constitutional Convention in Philadelphia, his wife did not go with him. "Mrs. Washington is become too Domestick, and too attentive to two little Grand Children to leave home," George Washington wrote to a friend.[6] He did not feel like leaving Mount

Vernon either, but he feared America was reaching a crisis point.[7] The Articles of Confederation, the first agreement that bound the states together, had not created a strong national government. Congress could not levy taxes, maintain an army, or settle border disputes between states. Washington felt the government needed more power if the new nation was to solve its problems successfully.

Reading the letters her husband wrote home, Martha Washington must have been both proud and apprehensive to learn that he had been chosen to be president of the convention. She hoped that his involvement with politics would not interfere with his home life more than was absolutely necessary.[8]

George Washington spent the summer of 1787 helping to hammer out the details of the proposed Constitution, which provided for separate executive, legislative, and judicial branches of government. He did not arrive home again until September 22. As George Washington slipped back into his country routine, Congress prepared to send the Constitution to the state legislatures for consideration. At least nine states had to ratify the Constitution before it could go into effect.

Although George Washington took no part in the debates, state legislators thought about him as they discussed the merits of the new Constitution. They definitely had plans for the general's future. In June 1788, New Hampshire became the ninth state to approve the Constitution. Soon Virginia, New York, North Carolina, and Rhode Island also voted in favor of the Constitution. As pleased as her husband was at this outcome, Martha Washington must have seen that something else preyed on his mind.[9] Elections for senators and representatives still had to be held. Washington was anxious for Federalists (supporters of the Constitution and a strong central government) to defeat their Anti-Federalist opponents (champions of powerful state governments).[10]

The Bill Of Rights

Many people worried that the proposed Constitution did not guarantee the basic rights of United States citizens. What about freedom of speech, freedom of religion, the right to a trial by jury, or the right to bear firearms? Federalists promised that if the Constitution were ratified, they would support additions to spell out these and other rights. They kept their promise, and on December 15, 1791, Virginia became the deciding state when it ratified the constitutional safeguards. These first ten amendments are known as the Bill of Rights.[11]

Even when the Federalists did win most of the congressional seats, a crucial question remained. Who would lead the new government? Perhaps Martha Washington was already steeling herself for another great change in her life. Neither the general nor his wife was surprised when a messenger arrived with momentous news.[12] The electoral college had unanimously selected George Washington to be the first president of the United States.

Martha Washington regarded the future with a mixture of pride, anxiety, and regret.[13] Life was good in Virginia. She had believed her days of travel were long behind her. But two days after the messenger's arrival, George Washington was on his way to the seat of government in New York. One month later, on May 16, 1789, Martha Washington, her grandchildren, and nephew Robert Lewis were ready to join him.

North to the New Capital

Several small adventures occurred on the road—a treacherous current that tugged at the ferry while they crossed the Potomac River, runaway horses that broke from the reins, another river crossing in which high waves dumped a great deal of water into the rocking boat. But these ordeals paled beside the excitement that greeted the travelers in Baltimore. A crowd cheered the carriage as it crossed the narrow streets to the house where Martha Washington and her party would stay. Fireworks and a band concert were staged in her honor. "To sleep was impossible . . ." wrote her nephew, "we were seranaded [entertained by musicians] until two o'clock in the morning."[14]

Philadelphia was even more extravagant in its welcome. Two military troops as well as several women in their carriages awaited her arrival. Once again, crowds cheered, bells rang, and a thirteen-gun salute echoed through the air. Martha Washington was so moved that she did something unheard of for a woman in eighteenth-century America. She made her first and only public speech. "She arose," according to one observer, "and standing in the carriage, thanked the troops who had escorted her, and the citizens also."[15] Later when Martha Washington tried to do a little shopping, she was recognized and hailed by well-wishers.[16] She could not even leave Philadelphia without a following of reporters.

Triumphant Arrival

Two days later, Martha Washington and her party arrived at Elizabethtown, New Jersey, where she, Nelly, and little Wash were reunited with the newly inaugurated President Washington. Amid great fanfare, they boarded the forty-seven-foot presidential barge that would take them across the water to New York. Thirteen uniformed men handled the oars while banners and flags flapped in the wind. A thirteen-gun salute marked the passage, and cries of "God bless Lady Washington" rose from the crowd.[17] If she had not realized it before, she knew now that her life would never again be the same.

Chapter 9

CREATING A NEW ROLE

Almost from the moment she arrived at her new home, Martha Washington was caught up in a whirlwind of activity. Her biggest concern was finding a good school for Nelly and Wash, but countless other demands were made on her. As the president's wife, she had to entertain important statesmen, welcome representatives from foreign countries, and help to establish tradition. The transformation from a private person into a public figure was sudden and bewildering. Although well-known and respected during the war, she had not been the focus of such intense attention.

But then so many things were confusing in the early days of George Washington's first term. The presidency was such a new office that proper etiquette for dealing with the chief executive still had to be established. Should he be given a fancy title like "His Elective Majesty" or "His Mightiness"? The issue was hotly debated by Congress as well as the newspapers.[1] No one wanted to treat the new president like a king, but no one wanted to slight him either.

"Remember the Ladies"

Abigail Adams, the second First Lady and the wife of the first vice president, is remembered for her strong views on women's rights. In 1776, she wrote to her husband, a delegate to the Continental Congress: "Remember the Ladies, and be more generous and favourable to them than your ancestors. Do not put such unlimited powers into the hands of the Husbands. . . . If perticuliar care and attention is not paid to the Laidies we are determined to foment a Rebelion, and will not hold ourselves bound by any Laws in which we have no voice, or Representation."[2] Although her words echoed the patriots' complaints against England, her warning was not heeded. Future generations of women would have to demand their own rights.

George Washington himself faced a dilemma when he tried to decide how to behave in his official role. A president had to be approachable, someone who listened and responded to the people. At the same time, he had to be formal, commanding dignity and respect. How was the country's first leader to achieve this important balance?

Martha Washington's Receptions

Martha Washington, too, was faced with the task of starting new, appropriate traditions as First Lady. Within days of her arrival, she held the first of her weekly receptions, or levees. Both men and women were welcome at these Friday evening affairs. Her husband, who attended as a guest, found it easier to relax and mingle at these events than he did at his own weekly receptions. While the president moved freely about the room, Martha Washington, usually dressed in white, sat on a sofa beside Abigail Adams, wife of Vice President John Adams.

Martha Washington's receptions tended to be staid affairs. But on one occasion, cries of alarm interrupted the patter of polite conversation. A lady with an especially large headdress had passed too close to the candles in a chandelier. Her carefully crafted headwear began to smolder. As men rushed to extinguish the flames, attention shifted from the First Lady to her unfortunate guest.

Even after such excitement, Martha Washington kept to decorum. In keeping with her custom, she rose at 9:00 P.M. and tactfully reminded the company, "The General always retires at nine, and I usually precede him."[3] It was time for the guests to depart.

Although Martha Washington's receptions were both formal and friendly, a few people felt they were too similar to the gatherings of English nobles. "Queenly drawing rooms," one newspaper said, dismissing her gatherings.[4] Another labeled them "our American Court!" and went on to charge that such gatherings weakened "republican principles."[5] Martha Washington even heard that some Virginians considered her receptions "awkward imitations of royalty."[6] Although she tried not to take the criticism personally, she must have been disappointed and a little puzzled by it. She considered the complaints carefully and tried to appear democratic in all her actions. Her receptions were open to all Americans, and it was important that people feel free to attend and enjoy them.

Determined to Be Cheerful

But what about her own freedom? Sometimes Martha Washington grew discouraged. "I live a very dull life hear and know nothing that passes in the town," she wrote to her niece Fanny in October 1789. "I think I am more like a state prisoner than anything else . . ."[7]

Yet such laments were not typical of Martha Washington. Just two months later she described her life to her friend Mercy Warren more positively. Admitting she would rather be home at Mount Vernon, she hastened to add,

> *I do not say this because I feel dissatisfied with my present station—no, God forbid:— . . . I am still determined to be cheerful and to be happy in whatever situation I may be, for I have also learnt from experiance that the greater part of our happiness or misery depends upon our dispositions, and not upon our circumstances; we carry the seeds of the one, or the other about with us, in our minds, wherever we go.*[8]

That kind of determination served Martha Washington well when the president required surgery just two months after her arrival. According to tradition, it was Martha Washington who had the street roped off to discourage curious visitors. She arranged to have the road covered with straw to deaden the noise of street traffic, and she stopped peddlers from calling out their wares.[9] She waited anxiously while doctors removed a large tumor from her husband's thigh. Surgery was a dangerous business in the days before painkillers and medicine to prevent infection. But Washington came through the procedure safely. As her husband regained strength, she went for rides with him, seeing to his comfort, while he lay full-length in the carriage. There was nothing she would not do to protect his health.

New Capital

Perhaps it was the record number of guests visiting the new president and First Lady that prompted the Washingtons to look for a bigger house. In 1790, they moved into another dwelling with a fine view of the Hudson River. They were not in the new home long before the president became seriously ill with a respiratory ailment.

After his recovery in the fall of 1790, the family went to Mount Vernon. No trip could have made Martha Washington happier. Two months later, when it was time to resume their public life, they left for Philadelphia, where the capital had moved in their absence. This was a city Martha Washington knew well from her Revolutionary War travels. She had many friends and felt more at home there than she had in New York. Once again, she held receptions on Friday nights, made social calls, and entertained a wide variety of guests in her home.

First Lady's Routine

Just as she had at Mount Vernon, Martha Washington rose early each day. Breakfast with her husband was followed by the same hour of privacy that she had always insisted upon. Fortified to face the day, Martha Washington emerged from her room and set off on a round of social calls. Often a formal dinner would be held in the evening for members of Congress. Martha Washington took care to make these occasions gracious and warm.

But Martha Washington's happiest moments were spent with her husband and grandchildren. Often they attended church together on Sunday and went for scenic carriage rides outside the city. They also enjoyed seeing plays. Wash never forgot how the audiences cried out for "Washington's March" whenever the president's family entered the theater.[10]

Even without her husband, Martha Washington attracted a great deal of attention.[11] Nelly, who enjoyed the excitement, thrived under her grandmother's watchful and loving eye. "[Grandmama] has been more than a Mother to me," she later wrote. "It is impossible to love anyone more than I love her."[12]

Happy Reunions

Sometimes soldiers visited the president's house, or "head-quarters," as they fondly referred to it.[13] Remembering their hardships and courage, Martha Washington felt she could never do enough to welcome these veterans. The men had come to count on her interest and generosity. When soldiers told her of their troubles, Martha Washington gave them a little money. But it was her ready sympathy and friendship that touched the veterans most.

George Washington's Second Term

On March 4, 1793, George Washington took the oath of office for a second term as president. At sixty-one, Martha Washington yearned for the peace and privacy of Mount Vernon more than ever. In one letter she even referred to her time in New York and Philadelphia as the "lost years."[14] Still, she was long accustomed to putting her duty before her wishes.[15] She continued to fulfill her social responsibilities with poise and grace.

President Washington faced many difficulties during the next four years. Arguments between Federalists, like himself, and Anti-Federalists, or Democratic-Republicans, like Thomas Jefferson, were sometimes heated. The president tried not to favor either party in his administration. He chose the best person for the job, regardless of politics. Sometimes this caused tension in the government.[16] Only George Washington's commanding presence could keep the two factions in check and the government running smoothly. Foreign affairs such as the French Revolution and British aggression toward American merchant ships occupied a great deal of the president's time.

On the home front, President Washington had to deal with the Whiskey Rebellion, in which angry whiskey makers refused to pay taxes. Rioters confronted the tax collectors and the soldiers who were sent to protect the tax collectors' property. Seven thousand rebels rallied outside Pittsburgh.

On September 30, 1794, the First Lady watched her husband's carriage set out for western Pennsylvania. Heading an army five times as big as the one he had led at Trenton, New Jersey, the president met no resistance as he visited several sites in Virginia and Pennsylvania. The Whiskey Rebellion was soon over, because its leaders backed down in the face of President Washington's show of force.

Enthusiastic American

Although she allowed no controversial talk at her receptions, Martha Washington could no longer ignore politics as she had tried to do at Mount Vernon. She read many newspapers, talked over current events with her husband, and tried to support all his views.[17] In public she kept her views to herself, but she made no secret of her love for America. "I think our country affords every

Another Revolution

During the French Revolution, the Bastille, a prison that symbolized royal tyranny, was destroyed. As a tribute to his former commander, the Marquis de Lafayette sent the prison key to George Washington, "from a Missionary of Liberty to its Patriarch." However, the French Revolution soon degenerated into a "reign of terror," in which many nobles—even those who supported freedom—were killed. Lafayette himself was forced to go into exile. For protection, his son George Washington Lafayette was sent to live in America with the Washingtons, who welcomed him as a son. The younger Lafayette returned to France in 1797.[18]

thing that can give pleasure or satisfaction to a rational mind," she told a friend.[19] Occasionally, she referred to politics in her letters. Mindful of her poor spelling, she sometimes dictated her correspondence to a secretary, then copied what he wrote in her own hand.[20] But her letters remained as honest and straightforward as everything else about her.

Throughout her years as First Lady, Martha Washington's stately simplicity and friendliness impressed everyone. "Her manners are modest and unassuming, dignified and femenine . . ." wrote Abigail Adams. "No lady can be more deservedly beloved and esteemed as she is. . . ."[21] Other guests echoed these feelings.

Shortly before President Washington left office in 1797, a ball was held to celebrate his birthday. Martha Washington's eyes filled with tears as she watched twelve thousand people cram into the amphitheater to honor her husband.[22] Less than two weeks later, John Adams was sworn in as the second president of the United States. At last, George and Martha Washington were going home.

Chapter 10

RELEASE

Martha Washington took to her old life as if she had never been away.[1] "The General and I feel like children just released from school or from a hard taskmaster," she wrote to a friend.[2] Despite her sixty-five years, she felt young again, as eager to create a comfortable, elegant home as she had been as a bride.

Even at Mount Vernon, many visitors arrived, hoping for a chance to greet the former president. Martha Washington, though relishing her rare moments of privacy, realized the public still had a claim on her husband. She welcomed her guests kindly.

Busy Matron

Just as she had done during the Revolutionary War, Martha Washington felt free to knit or sew while she chatted with her women guests.[3] Once, she gave away the very pair of gloves she was working on. She told her visitor to finish the gloves and wear them as a souvenir. Martha Washington could sew, supervise the servants' garment making, and teach a young slave to knit all at the same time.[4]

Times had certainly changed, but Martha Washington still thought of herself as "an old-fashioned Virginia housekeeper."[5]

She enjoyed planning meals; sitting on the veranda, which overlooked the Potomac; and caring for eighteen-year-old Nelly and sixteen-year-old Wash. "Steady as a clock, busy as a bee and as cheerful as a cricket," was how she described herself.[6] Very little could persuade Martha Washington to leave Mount Vernon, but the spring after her husband left office, she accompanied him sixteen miles north to the new federal city, which would later be named "Washington" after the first president.[7] She wanted to see the site of what would become the nation's capital, and she took a keen interest in real estate in the area.

Martha Washington's dearest concerns, however, were always closer to home. February 22, 1799, was an especially happy day. Her husband celebrated his sixty-seventh birthday, and Nelly Custis married George Washington's nephew, Lawrence Lewis, in a simple ceremony at Mount Vernon. On November 27, Nelly gave birth to Martha Washington's first great-grandchild, a little girl named Frances Parke.

If Not for Martha

Once, when George Washington tried to persuade a reluctant landowner to sell some property in the new federal city, he received a reply that must have amused him and Martha Washington, too. "I suppose you think people here are going to take every grist that comes from you as pure grain," said David Bruns, as if the former president expected to have his every word obeyed. Then Bruns added, "What would you have been if you hadn't married the widow Custis?"[8]

George Washington's Death

As had often happened in Martha Washington's life, sorrow swiftly followed joy. Less than two weeks after the baby's arrival, George Washington spent several hours riding around the plantation in a freezing rainstorm. He became seriously ill with what was probably a bacterial throat infection. Doctors could not stop the course of his illness. For nearly twenty-four hours, Martha Washington stayed by her husband's side. On December 14, 1799, George Washington died.

Although she had remained calm at his bedside, Martha Washington was too emotionally shattered to attend the funeral.[9] She closed up the sunny bedroom she had shared with her husband and moved to a narrow attic room with a single dormer window. It is said that she never again entered the room where her husband died.[10]

A New Attitude Toward Slavery

George Washington's experiences fighting a war and leading a nation had caused him to rethink his position as a slaveholder. He became "principled against selling Negroes, as you would cattle in the market" and resolved, if at all possible, "never again to become the master of another slave by purchase."[11] In his will, the former president provided for the freeing of his slaves at the time of his wife's death. Practical considerations of keeping slave families together prevented him from doing this earlier. The executors of his will were to provide for the elderly slaves and to teach the young to read and write.[12]

Packages and letters of condolence poured into Mount Vernon. In fact, so much mail arrived that Congress passed a special act just for Martha Washington. She was given the franking privilege, which meant she could mail letters without paying for stamps. By this time, Martha Washington was a legend in her own right, and visitors came to Mount Vernon especially to see her. She was their living link to a time of great patriotism and triumph, and they were her window to a rapidly changing America. Her interest in politics remained strong, and she welcomed her visitors with the same hospitality of happier days. "Her countenance [is] very little wrinkled and remarkably fair for a person of her years," one visitor noted. "She appeared as much rejoiced at receiving our visit as if we had been of her nearest connections."[13]

Final Days

In August 1801, Martha Washington's second great-granddaughter and namesake, Martha Betty Lewis, was born. Martha Washington doted on the children and cherished signs of their love.[14] She remained the heart of her family, a source of moral strength and inspiration. But her health had begun to fail. She knew the fascination with America's first president, "the Father of Our Country," would not end with her death. For years, Martha Washington had sacrificed her privacy. Some things, however, were too personal to risk sharing. To ensure her privacy, she burned George Washington's letters to her. Only two are known to exist today.[15]

Martha Washington had clearly had enough of fame and public image. Although her official portrait had been painted a number of times, she wanted a different legacy for her family. Tradition says she asked artist Robert Field to paint her "plain everyday face" so her grandchildren could remember her the way she really was.[16] She felt they did not need another formal portrait that flattered her and emphasized her dignity.

Nelly was heartbroken as her grandmother's health continued to fail. In her little attic bedroom, Martha Washington calmly read the Bible and knitted. She enjoyed Nelly's presence and the hymns her granddaughter sometimes sang for her.[17] In the spring, a severe fever weakened her further. On May 22, 1802, Martha Washington died at the age of seventy.

Chapter 11

BELOVED LADY

A fter her husband's death, Martha Washington had lived to see the removal of the nation's capital from Philadelphia to the new federal city at Washington, D.C. She had seen Thomas Jefferson, her husband's political adversary, elected to the presidency, an event she called "The greatest misfortune the country has ever experienced."[1]

In another age, Martha Washington might have supported the right of women to help elect the president. But she accepted the limits imposed on eighteenth-century women, doing exactly what was expected of her with courage and dignity. Unfailingly, she sacrificed her own comfort and peace of mind for the American cause.

Martha Washington's legacy was more personal than political. She enjoyed people and knew intuitively how to make them feel at home. Her comforting presence at wartime camps allowed her husband to focus his attention on military issues. From foreign dignitaries to the humblest soldier, Martha Washington spread hope and serenity, even in desperate times.

The soldiers never forgot the comfort and cheer she brought them. Even after George Washington became president, many felt free to visit Martha Washington and share their cares.

Political Parties

Although Thomas Jefferson served as secretary of state under George Washington, he disagreed with the president's Federalist policies. He was more concerned with individual liberty than with a strong central government. Although President Washington had liked and respected Jefferson, he eventually became deeply disappointed in his fellow Virginian. In 1797, American newspapers printed a letter in which Jefferson called the Federalists "the Anglican, monarchical, and aristocratical party." It is not surprising that a staunch Federalist like Martha Washington bewailed his election.[2]

Delighted, the First Lady welcomed Revolutionary War veterans as old friends. Her actions to promote their well-being earned praise from the veterans and set a precedent for other First Ladies to support worthy causes.[3]

Martha Washington left her stamp not only on the role of First Lady, but on the presidency itself. Her winning combination of elegance and warmth helped strike the right balance between formality and familiarity during America's first presidential administration.[4] In this way, she helped define a distinctly American style of leadership that is both strong and sensitive to public opinion. Her receptions contributed to the public's dual perception of her husband's position: He was the country's chief executive, but at the same time he was a fellow American.

What Comes from the Heart

Perhaps Martha Washington summed up her personal legacy best when she wrote early in her husband's presidency, "I am fond only of what comes from the heart."[5] Whatever she could do to further the cause of independence or to strengthen the new nation, Martha Washington did with a loyal, caring heart. By temperament as well as by marriage, this brave and generous lady was well-suited to be the "Mother of Our Country."

Martha Washington's patriotism, sensitivity, and enormous strength of character won her great respect and affection. "She was the worthy partner of the worthiest of men," declared an Alexandria newspaper at her death.[6] Another newspaper referred to Martha Washington's "dignity of manners" and "superiority of understanding."[7] But the greatest praise of all came from a former Mount Vernon slave. Speaking "from the heart," like the First Lady herself, he summed up her character by saying: "The general was only a man, but Mrs. Washington was perfect."[8]

CHRONOLOGY

1731—Born, New Kent County, Virginia, on June 2.

1750—Marries Colonel Daniel Parke Custis on May 15.

1751—Son Daniel Parke Custis II born in November.

1753—Daughter Frances Parke Custis born on April 12.

1754—Son Daniel dies on February 19.

1755—Son John Parke Custis (Jacky) born.

1756—Daughter Martha Parke Custis (Patcy) born.

1757—Daughter Frances dies; Husband Daniel Parke Custis dies on July 8.

1759—Marries Colonel George Washington on January 6; Arrives at Mount Vernon in April.

1773—Daughter Martha (Patcy) dies on June 19.

1774—Son John (Jacky) marries Eleanor (Nelly) Calvert on February 3.

1775—George Washington commissioned as commander in chief of the American forces; Arrives in November at Cambridge, Massachusetts, to spend the winter at military headquarters.

1776—Declaration of Independence is signed.

1777—Arrives in March at Morristown, New Jersey; Joins George Washington in early November at Valley Forge.

1778—Joins George Washington at winter headquarters in Middlebrook, New Jersey.

1779—Arrives by December at winter headquarters in Morristown, New Jersey.

1780—Arrives by December at winter headquarters at New Windsor, New York.

1781—Son Jacky Custis dies of camp fever after the Battle of Yorktown; Accompanies George Washington to Philadelphia on November 28.

1782—Accompanies George Washington to headquarters in Newburgh, New York.

1783—Arrives in August at Princeton, New Jersey, headquarters; Watches George Washington resign his military commission at Annapolis, Maryland, on December 19; Unofficially adopts two youngest grandchildren, Eleanor Parke Custis (Nelly) and George Washington Parke Custis (Wash), after the remarriage of their mother.

1789—Joins new President George Washington in New York.

1790—United States capital moves from New York to Philadelphia.

1793—George Washington inaugurated for second term as president.

1797—Returns to private life at Mount Vernon.

1799—George Washington dies on December 14.

1802—Martha Washington dies on May 22.

CHAPTER NOTES

Chapter 1. Pattern of Industry

1. Anne Hollingsworth Wharton, *Martha Washington* (New York: Charles Scribner's Sons, 1897), p. 114.

2. Elswyth Thane, *Washington's Lady* (New York: Duell, Sloan and Pearce, 1960), p. 151.

3. Christine Meadows, "George Washington: Founding Father," A & E Video Biography, 1994.

4. Douglas Southall Freeman, *George Washington: A Biography, Leader of the Revolution* (New York: Charles Scribner's Sons, 1951), vol. 4, p. 382.

5. Russell F. Weigley, "The Morristown Encampments and the American Revolution," *Morristown: Official National Park Handbook* (Washington, D.C.: U.S. Department of the Interior, 1983), p. 44.

6. Weigley, p. 38.

7. Margaret C. Conkling, *Memoirs of the Mother and Wife of Washington* (New York and Auburn: Miller, Orton & Mulligan, 1855), pp. 153–154; Mary Wells Ashworth, *Martha Washington: The First Lady* (Mount Vernon, Va.: Mount Vernon Ladies' Association, 1960), pp. 4–5.

8. Wharton, p. 116.

9. Ibid., p. 117; Thane, p. 158.

10. Conkling, p. 143.

11. Ibid.

12. Wharton, p. 113; Thane, p. 158.

Chapter 2. Martha Dandridge Custis

1. Polly Longworth, "Portrait of Martha, Belle of New Kent," *Colonial Williamsburg*, Summer 1988, p. 4.

2. Ibid., p. 6.

3. Paul F. Boller, Jr., *Presidential Wives* (New York; Oxford: Oxford University Press, 1988), p. 8; Marianne Means, *The Woman in the White House* (New York: 1963), p. 19.

4. Edmund S. Morgan, *Virginians at Home: Family Life in the Eighteenth Century* (Williamsburg, Va.: Colonial Williamsburg, Inc., 1952), p. 18.

5. Longworth, p. 6.

6. Joseph E. Fields, comp., *"Worthy Partner," The Papers of Martha Washington* (Westport, Conn.; London: Greenwood Press, 1984), pp. 421, 427.

7. Benson J. Lossing, *Mary and Martha: The Mother and Wife of George Washington* (New York: Harper & Brothers, 1886), p. 84.

8. Douglas Southall Freeman, *George Washington: A Biography, Young Washington* (New York: Charles Scribners' Sons, 1948), vol. 2, p. 297.

9. Fields, pp. 430, 434.

10. Ibid., p. 432; Lossing, p. 88.

11. Fields, pp. 440, 434.

12. Ibid., p. 3.

13. Ivor Noel Humes, "Custis Square: The Williamsburg Home and Garden of a Very Curious Gentleman," *Colonial Williamsburg*, Summer 1994, p. 25.

14. Longworth, p. 11.

15. Fields, p. 437.

Chapter 3. Enter a Young Soldier

1. Douglas Southall Freeman, *George Washington: A Biography, Young Washington* (New York: Charles Scribner's Sons, 1948), vol. 2, p. 404.

2. James Thomas Flexner, *Washington: The Indispensable Man* (Boston: Little, Brown and Company, 1969), p. 36.

3. George Washington Parke Custis, *Recollections and Private Memories of Washington* (Philadelphia: William Flint, 1860), p. 500.

4. Flexner, p. 41.

5. Richard Brookhiser, *Founding Father: Rediscovering George Washington* (New York: Simon & Schuster, 1996), p. 23.

6. Freeman, p. 399.

7. Douglas Southall Freeman, *George Washington: A Biography, Planter and Patriot* (New York: Charles Scribner's Sons, 1951), vol. 3, p. 1.

8. Washington Irving, *George Washington: A Biography*, ed. Charles Neider (New York: DaCapo Press, 1994), p. 111.

9. Freeman, vol. 3, p. 15.

10. Miriam Anne Bourne, *First Family: George Washington and His Intimate Relations* (New York; London: W. W. Norton & Company, 1982), p. 21.

11. Anne Hollingsworth Wharton, *Martha Washington* (New York: Charles Scribner's Sons, 1897), p. 53.

12. Mary Wells Ashworth, "Martha Washington: The First Lady," *Mount Vernon Ladies' Association Annual Report* (Mount Vernon, Va.: Mount Vernon Ladies' Association, 1960), p. 3.

13. Bourne, p. 22.

14. W. W. Abbot and Dorothy Twohig, eds., *The Papers of George Washington, Confederation Series* (Charlottesville; London: University Press of Virginia, 1995), vol. 4, p. 105.

15. Flexner, p. 52.

16. W. W. Abbott and Dorothy Twohig, eds., *The Papers of George Washington, Colonial Series* (Charlottesville: University Press of Virginia, 1988), vol. 6, p. 359.

17. Freeman, vol. 3, p. 2.

18. Joseph E. Fields, comp., *"Worthy Partner," The Papers of Martha Washington* (Westport, Conn.; London: Greenwood Press, 1994), p. 147.

Chapter 4. Trouble on the Horizon

1. Elswyth Thane, *Washington's Lady* (New York: Duell, Sloan and Pearce, 1960), p. 40.

2. Ibid., p. 51.

3. Donald Jackson and Dorothy Twohig, eds., *The Diaries of George Washington* (Charlottesville: University Press of Virginia, 1976), vol. 2, p. 68.

4. Ibid., p. 141.

5. Webb Garrison, *Great Stories of the American Revolution* (Nashville, Tenn.: Rutledge Hill Press, 1990), pp. 36–37.

6. Douglas Southall Freeman, *George Washington: A Biography, Planter and Patriot* (New York: Charles Scribner's Sons, 1951), vol. 3, p. 211.

Chapter 5. Spartan Mother

1. Donald Jackson and Dorothy Twohig, eds., *The Diaries of George Washington* (Charlottesville: University Press of Virginia, 1976), vol. 2, p. 257.

2. Elswyth Thane, *Washington's Lady* (New York: Duell, Sloan and Pearce, 1960), p. 67.

3. Jackson and Twohig, vol. 3, p. 188.

4. Miriam Anne Bourne, *First Family: George Washington and His Intimate Relations* (New York; London: W.W. Norton & Company, 1982), p. 37.

5. Thane, p. 74.

6. Eric Foner and John A. Garraty, eds., *The Reader's Companion to American History* (Boston: Houghton Mifflin Company, 1991), p. 125.

7. Thane, p. 75.

8. Ibid., p. 78.

9. Ibid.

10. William Wirt Henry, *Patrick Henry: Life, Correspondence and Speeches* (New York: Charles Scribner's Sons, 1892), vol. 1, p. 213.

11. Ibid.

12. Ibid.

13. John R. Alden, *George Washington: A Biography* (Baton Rouge; London: Louisiana State University Press, 1984), p. 106.

14. Webb Garrison, *Great Stories of the American Revolution* (Nashville, Tenn.: Rutledge Hill Press, 1990), p. 136.

15. Richard Brookhiser, *Founding Father: Rediscovering George Washington* (New York: Simon & Schuster, 1996), p. 22.

16. W.W. Abbott and Dorothy Twohig, eds., *The Papers of George Washington, Revolutionary War Series* (Charlottesville; London: University Press of Virginia, 1985), vol. 1, p. 3.

17. Ibid., pp. 3–4.

Chapter 6. Independence

1. Miriam Anne Bourne, *First Family: George Washington and His Intimate Relations* (New York; London: W. W. Norton & Company, 1982), p. 62.

2. Anne Hollingsworth Wharton, *Martha Washington* (New York: Charles Scribner's Sons, 1897), p. 95.

3. Joseph E. Fields, comp., *"Worthy Partner," The Papers of Martha Washington* (Westport, Conn.; London: Greenwood Press, 1994), p. 164.

4. Robert McHenry, ed., *Famous American Women: A Biographical Dictionary from Colonial Times to the Present* (New York: Dover Publications, Inc., 1980), p. 437.

5. Elswyth Thane, *Washington's Lady* (New York: Duell, Sloan and Pearce, 1960), p. 109.

6. McHenry, p. 431.

7. W.W. Abbott and Dorothy Twohig, eds., *The Papers of George Washington, Revolutionary War Series* (Charlottesville; London: University Press of Virginia, 1984), vol. 4, p. 435.

8. In *The Spark of Independence* (New York: History Book Club, 1997), p. 159.

9. Thane, p. 140.

10. Douglas Southall Freeman, *George Washington: A Biography, Leader of the Revolution* (New York: Charles Scribner's Sons, 1951), vol. 4, p. 194.

11. Eric Foner and John A. Garraty, eds., *The Reader's Companion to American History* (Boston: Houghton Mifflin Company, 1991), p. 271.

12. Thane, pp. 141–142.

Chapter 7. Victory and Sorrow

1. Benson J. Lossing, *Mary and Martha: The Mother and Wife of George Washington* (New York: Harper & Brothers, 1886), pp. 168, 171.

2. Ibid., p. 176.

3. Douglas Southall Freeman, *George Washington: A Biography, Victory With the Help of France* (New York: Charles Scribner's Sons, 1951), vol. 5, pp. 31, 33.

4. Washington Irving, *George Washington: A Biography*, ed. Charles Neider (New York: DaCapo Press, 1994), p. 562.

5. Miriam Anne Bourne, *First Family: George Washington and His Intimate Relations* (New York; London: W. W. Norton & Company, 1982), p. 84.

6. Donald Jackson and Dorothy Twohig, eds., *The Diaries of George Washington* (Charlottesville: University Press of Virginia, 1976), vol. 3, p. 425.

7. Charles Cecil Wall, *George Washington, Citizen-Soldier* (Mount Vernon, Va.: Mount Vernon Ladies' Association, 1994), p. 190.

8. Bourne, p. 95.

9. Patt Gibbs, comp., *Martha Dandridge Custis Chronology*, Colonial Williamsburg Foundation, February 1995, p. 5.

10. Irving, p. 620.

11. Eric Foner and John A. Garraty, eds., *The Reader's Companion to American History* (Boston: Houghton Mifflin Company, 1991), p. 823.

Chapter 8. God Bless Lady Washington

1. Charles Parmer, "Close-up of the First Lady," *The New York Times Magazine*, February 12, 1957, p. 12.

2. Donald Jackson and Dorothy Twohig, eds., *The Diaries of George Washington* (Charlottesville: University Press of Virginia, 1976), vol. 4, p. 156.

3. Miriam Anne Bourne, *First Family: George Washington and His Intimate Relations* (New York; London: W. W. Norton & Company, 1982), p. 100.

4. Anne Hollingsworth Wharton, *Martha Washington* (New York: Charles Scribner's Sons, 1887), p. 170.

5. Joseph E. Fields, comp., *"Worthy Partner," The Papers of Martha Washington* (Westport, Conn.; London: Greenwood Press, 1994), p. 205.

6. W.W. Abbott and Dorothy Twohig, eds., *The Papers of George Washington, Confederation Series* (Charlottesville; London: University Press of Virginia), vol. 5, p. 171.

7. Douglas Southall Freeman, *George Washington: A Biography, Patriot and President* (New York: Charles Scribner's Sons, 1954), vol. 6, p. 82.

8. Elswyth Thane, *Washington's Lady* (New York: Duell, Sloan and Pearce, 1960), p. 266.

9. Ralph K. Andrist, ed., *The Founding Fathers, George Washington: A Biography in His Own Words* (New York: Newsweek, 1972), p. 290.

10. Andrist, p. 290.

11. Eric Foner and John A. Garraty, eds., *The Reader's Companion to American History* (Boston: Houghton Mifflin Company, 1991), pp. 98–99.

12. Thane, p. 270.

13. Fields, p. 223.

14. Robert Lewis, "Sidelights: A Journey from Fredericksburg, Virginia to New York," *Maryland Historical Magazine*, June 1958, p. 185.

15. Carl Sferrazza Anthony, *First Ladies: The Saga of the Presidents' Wives and Their Power, 1789–1961* (New York: William Morrow, 1990), p. 38.

16. Ibid.

17. Ibid.

Chapter 9. Creating a New Role

1. W. W. Abbott and Dorothy Twohig, eds., *The Papers of George Washington, Presidential Series* (Charlottesville: University Press of Virginia, 1987), vol. 2, p. 249.

2. Vincent Wilson, Jr., *The Book of Distinguished American Women* (Brookville, Md.: American History Research Associates, 1983), p. 10.

3. Anne Hollingsworth Wharton, *Martha Washington* (New York: Charles Scribner's Sons, 1897), p. 197.

4. Carl Sferrazza Anthony, *First Ladies: The Saga of the Presidents' Wives and Their Power, 1789–1961* (New York: William Morrow, 1990), p. 48.

5. Ibid.

6. Ibid.

7. Joseph E. Fields, comp., *"Worthy Partner," The Papers of Martha Washington* (Westport, Conn.; London: Greenwood Press, 1994), p. 220.

8. Ibid., pp. 223–224.

9. Anthony, pp. 43–44.

10. Miriam Anne Bourne, *First Family: George Washington and His Intimate Relations* (New York; London: W. W. Norton & Company, 1982), p. 130.

11. Margaret Truman, *First Ladies* (New York: Random House, 1955), p. 20.

12. Patricia Brady, ed., *George Washington's Beautiful Nelly: The Letters of Eleanor Parke Custis to Elizabeth Bordley Gibson, 1794–1851* (Columbia, S.C.: University of South Carolina Press, 1991), p. 20.

13. Benson J. Lossing, *Mary and Martha: The Mother and Wife of George Washington* (New York: Harper & Brothers, 1886), p. 291.

14. Mary Wells Ashworth, *Martha Washington: The First First Lady* (Mount Vernon, Va.: Mount Vernon Ladies' Association, 1960), p. 6.

15. Ibid., p. 8.

16. John R. Alden, *George Washington: A Biography* (Baton Rouge; London: Louisiana State University Press, 1984), p. 296.

17. Anthony, p. 50.

18. David L. Ribblett, *Nelly Custis: Child of Mount Vernon* (Mount Vernon, Va.: Mount Vernon Ladies' Association, 1993), p. 31.

19. Fields, p. 229.

20. Anthony, p. 40.

21. Bourne, p. 129.

22. Ibid., p. 172.

Chapter 10. Release

1. Miriam Anne Bourne, *First Family: George Washington and His Intimate Relations* (New York; London: W.W. Norton & Company, 1982), p. 173.

2. Joseph E. Fields, comp., *"Worthy Partner," The Papers of Martha Washington* (Westport, Conn.; London: Greenwood Press, 1994), p. 303.

3. Bourne, p. 195.

4. Anne Hollingsworth Wharton, *Martha Washington* (New York: Charles Scribner's Sons, 1897), p. 277.

5. Fields, p. 304.

6. Ibid.

7. Donald Jackson and Dorothy Twohig, eds., *The Diaries of George Washington* (Charlottesville: University Press of Virginia, 1979), vol. 6, p. 297.

8. Laura C. Holloway, *The Ladies of the White House, or, In the Home of the Presidents* (Philadelphia: A. Gorton & Co., 1882), p. 67.

9. David Ribblett, *Nelly Custis: Child of Mount Vernon* (Mount Vernon, Va.: Mount Vernon Ladies' Association, 1993), p. 50.

10. Ibid., p. 52.

11. John Alexander Carroll and Mary Wells Ashworth, *George Washington: A Biography, First in Peace* (New York: Charles Scribner's Sons, 1957), vol. 7, p. 585.

12. John R. Alden, *George Washington: A Biography* (Baton Rouge; London: Louisiana State University Press, 1984), p. 303.

13. Fields, p. xxvii.

14. Ribblett, p. 52.

15. Fields, p. xxxi.

16. Lauren Suber, "The Many Faces of Martha Washington," *Colonial Williamsburg*, Spring 1995, p. 68.

17. Ribblett, p. 52.

Chapter 11. Beloved Lady

1. David L. Ribblett, *Nelly Custis: Child of Mount Vernon* (Mount Vernon, Va.: Mount Vernon Ladies' Association, 1993), p. 51.

2. John R. Alden, *George Washington: A Biography* (Baton Rouge; London: Louisiana State University Press, 1984), p. 297.

3. Carl Sferrazza Anthony, *First Ladies: The Saga of the Presidents' Wives and their Power, 1789–1961* (New York: William Morrow, 1990), p. 54.

4. Margaret Truman, *First Ladies* (New York: Random House, 1995), p. 21.

5. Joseph E. Fields, comp., *"Worthy Partner," The Papers of Martha Washington* (Westport, Conn.; London: Greenwood Press, 1994), p. 223.

6. Ibid., p. xxvii.

7. Anne Hollingsworth Wharton, *Martha Washington* (New York: Charles Scribner's Sons, 1897), p. 286.

8. Fields, p. xix.

GLOSSARY

Anti-Federalist—Political party that opposed adoption of the United States Constitution in 1787–1788.

Articles of Confederation—The agreement that bound the original thirteen states together into a loose union.

Bill of Rights—First ten amendments to the United States Constitution, which guarantee personal liberties such as freedom of speech and freedom of religion.

Constitutional Convention—Body of representatives from twelve of the thirteen states that met in Philadelphia in 1787 to develop a more workable constitution.

Continental Congress—Representatives from twelve of the thirteen colonies who first met in 1774 to formulate ways to deal with British oppression.

Declaration of Independence—Resolution adopted by the Continental Congress in 1776 that severed American political ties with England.

democracy—Government in which the people have a direct say or elect representatives to speak for them.

electoral college—Group of representatives from each state that meets to elect the president and vice president.

executive—Branch of government that administers the laws.

Federalist—Political party in favor of a strong central government.

House of Burgesses—Elected body of the Virginia Assembly; the governing body in colonial Virginia.

inoculation—A way to confer immunity to a disease, such as smallpox, by introducing a small amount of the virus into a person or animal and stimulating the production of antibodies.

judicial—Branch of government that interprets the laws.

legislative—Branch of government that makes the laws.

monarchy—Government ruled by a hereditary king or monarch.

protocol—Formal procedure used in government or military affairs.

ratify—To approve a system of government, constitutional amendment, or foreign treaty.

Stamp Act—Law passed by the English Parliament in 1765 that required Americans to buy stamps for all public documents, including newspapers.

Tea Act—A measure passed by the English Parliament in 1773 that gave the East India Tea Company a monopoly in the American tea market.

Townshend Acts—Measures imposed by the English Parliament in 1767 that imposed taxes on a variety of goods, including paper, paint, tea, and glass.

Treaty of Paris—Treaty that ended the Revolutionary War.

FURTHER READING

Ashby, Ruth. *George and Martha Washington: Presidents and First Ladies.* New York: Gareth Stevens Publishing, 2004.

Brady, Patricia. *Martha Washington: An American Life.* New York: Viking, 2005.

Hakim, Joy. *A History of US: From Colonies to Country 1735–1791.* New York: Oxford University Press, 2006.

Haugen, Brenda. *Martha Washington: First Lady of the United States.* New York: Capstone, 2005.

Marrin, Albert. *George Washington and the Founding of a Nation.* New York: Dutton Juvenile, 2003.

Murray, Stuart. *American Revolution.* New York: DK Children, 2005.

INDEX

Westminster Public Library
3705 W. 112th Ave.
Westminster, CO 80031
www.westminsterlibrary.org